The Story of

Modern France

The Kings, the French Revolution, the Napoleonic Wars and the Establishment of Democracy and Liberty

By Hélène Adeline Guerber

PANTIANOS
CLASSICS

Published by Pantianos Classics

ISBN-13: 978-1-78987-243-9

First published in 1910

Contents

Preface

The aim of this volume is to give a complete graphic account of the main features of the history of France since 1715 A.D., with as much additional illuminating detail as limited space permits. Besides outlines of the principal events, this narrative includes many biographical sketches, together with the anecdotes and sayings to which allusions are often made in literature, politics, and art. It also gives such data in regard to places, public buildings, and works of art as the well informed like to have at their fingers' ends. As the work is intended mainly for youthful readers, due regard has been paid to moral teachings and to the judicious omission of harmful incidents.

The book is arranged for elementary history classes, and for supplementary reading as well. Some acquaintance with the history of France is most helpful in understanding and studying literature, and English, American, Medieval, and General history. Besides, in schools where French is taught, it can serve as a work of reference for the pupils, who continually stumble across names and allusions which require elucidation. The author, therefore, hopes many schools will find this narrative useful in one or the other conception, and that it will appeal equally to teachers and pupils and perhaps to other readers also.

Although complete in itself, and hence quite independent, it is nevertheless a sequel to *The Story of Old France*, for it takes up the thread of the narrative at the point where it was dropped in that book, and carries it on unbroken to the present date.

Many names occur and recur in the text because familiarity with their appearance is desirable from an educational point of view. Where the pronunciation seems difficult, it has been carefully indicated the first time the name appears, and the indication is repeated in the index. Before the day's reading, a few minutes may profitably be given to the pronunciation of such names by the teacher, with their repetition by the pupils. This process will facilitate the reading and hence increase the interest. Names in parenthesis need not be read aloud, sight acquaintance with them being all that is expected of young readers.

Conciergerie Sainte Chapelle | Notre Dame Institute Pantheon

Louvre

Seine River

The Central Part of Modern Paris.

7

The Old Monarchy

The most thrilling and important events in the history of France are those which have occurred within the last two hundred years, about which you will read in this book. But to know the condition of France, and how it was governed two centuries ago, it is well to begin with a brief review of previous events.

Stretching from the Atlantic Ocean to the Alps, and from the Pyrenees almost to the Rhine, France has long held a leading place in the history of Europe. The French are descended in part from the Gauls,—a half-civilized people—who gave their name to the country two thousand years ago, and from various other nations who, at different times, made their way into the land.

Greatest among these invaders were the Romans, who conquered Gaul before the Christian era, gave it their Latin language and civilization, and made it one of the important divisions of the great Roman Empire. The barbarian invaders—Goths, Vandals, Burgundians, Franks, and others—in the fifth century destroyed much of the work done by the Romans, and broke the country up into petty states. Then the whole land was gradually conquered by the Franks, a Germanic tribe from which France derives its present name, and some of its aristocratic families. But the French language contains mainly Latin and Gallic elements, and has few from other sources.

The conversion and baptism of the first great Frankish ruler, Clovis (496), earned for him and for his successors the proud title of "Eldest Son of the Church," and made France the Catholic country it has been ever since. The greatest of all Frankish monarchs, Charlemagne, ruled wisely and well over a vast empire, which included France, Belgium, the Netherlands, Switzerland, most of Germany and Italy, and part of Austria (800-814). Under his descendants this empire was repeatedly divided and reunited, but before long France became independent, while the other lands remained in the Empire, under German Emperors, for many centuries.

During this period the country suffered greatly from frequent struggles between rival kings and from constant disputes between monarch and nobles, each of whom wished to rule his share of land independently. Finally one of these nobles, more powerful than the rest—Hugh Capet (carpet, or, caper)—became King of France (987) and established his capital at Paris, which has ever since been the center of the French government.

Hugh Capet was the founder of the Capetian dynasty, which includes all of the later kings of France, and which two hundred years ago was at the height of its power. This dynasty respected the "Salic Law," by which the Franks decreed that the French throne should pass to males only; that is why no queen has ever reigned over France.

The throne of the Capetian kings was claimed at times by monarchs of other countries, but never successfully. For about one hundred years (1337–1453) France was devastated by kings of England who tried to gain the French crown in addition to their own. During that time the English held large parts of the country, but they were at last driven, from French soil by the efforts of Joan of Arc, whose heroic example rekindled dying patriotism in France.

The throne was again in danger during the Religious Wars (1562–1598), for, although less than one tenth of the population was Protestant, among that tenth was the king, Henry IV., the first of the Bourbon branch of the Capetian family. The majority of the French refused him obedience until he changed his faith and became a Catholic.

At first the power of the Capetian rulers was not great, because the people of France, by the old feudal system, owed allegiance to their lords. These lords, it is true, were vassals in turn to the king, but if a noble chose to rebel he could generally count on the support of the people in his own domain. In the Empire, many nobles thus succeeded in becoming petty monarchs, but in France the king gradually grew strong enough to enforce obedience from his vassals, and to keep the land one united country.

The first real French king, Hugh Capet, was himself a powerful noble, and his successors gradually increased the royal domain through conquest, marriage, inheritance, and purchase, until they became direct masters of the whole realm. Still, parts of these royal domains were sometimes granted to favorites or relatives, and thus the ranks of the nobles were recruited from princes of the royal blood. Under weak monarchs the great lords were at times nearly independent, but strong kings were able to exact submission, and in the end Louis XIV., third ruler of the Bourbon line, made himself an absolute monarch.

In the Middle Ages, besides king, nobles, and peasants—tillers of the soil—there grew up a merchant and manufacturing class, which collected in cities. Many of these centers soon purchased certain rights of self-government from nobles and kings, but these rights did not extend beyond the city limits. French burghers *(bourgeois)* never exercised any such influence in national affairs as was gained by the same class in England.

Unlike the English Parliament, French bodies bearing that name were simple courts of justice, composed of the lawyers and judges of certain towns, each of which had a separate parliament. The duty of each parliament was to "register" the decrees of the king, and see them properly enforced in a certain section of the country. Occasionally the parliaments—especially that of Paris—protested against unpopular decrees and exerted some little influence in lawmaking by delaying or refusing to register them. But Louis XIV. commanded his parliaments to register every decree of his without discussion or delay, and he was obeyed.

The only national assembly in France—the States-General—met only at the call of the king and had no real power. It consisted of the three divisions or estates of society: the Nobles, entitled to sit in it by right of birth; the Clergy, by right of office; and the Burghers, representatives of the Commons or Third Estate. The States-General had met fifteen times by 1614, but during Louis XIV.'s long reign (1643–1715) he never summoned this body. It met only once thereafter, a most momentous meeting, as you will see.

In the early part of Louis XIV.'s reign was reached the high water mark of prosperity under the Old Regime, or absolute monarchy. It was this king who built the great palace of Versailles, and gathered there the most magnificent court in Europe. But the glories of the age of Louis XIV. were greatly dimmed by useless wars and by boundless extravagance, in which he was closely imitated by his nobles. As a result, the state was burdened with an immense debt, the taxes were greatly increased, and the Third Estate—the only class paying direct taxes—was reduced to dire poverty. General discontent naturally ensued, which set in motion the thrilling series of events which overthrew the old monarchy and gave birth to modern France.

The Minority of Louis XV.

When Louis XIV. breathed his last (1715), the most unseemly rejoicings took place, for every one was delighted that his seventy-two years' reign was at an end, and expected great things from his successor. Not only were the late king's remains insulted on their way to the Abbey of St. Denis, but his carefully drawn-up will was annulled—as, indeed, he had foreseen it would be. In fact, the five-year-old Louis XV. (great-grandson of Louis XIV.) was taken to the Parliament of Paris for the first time on purpose to have this will revoked, and to have a nephew of. Louis XIV., namely Philip, the Duke of Orleans, appointed regent of the realm during the new king's minority, instead of the persons named in the will.

So that things may be quite clear, you must bear in mind that if Louis XV. were to die before marrying and having a son to succeed him, the crown

Philip, Duke of Orleans.

would naturally pass to his nearest male relative. But this nearest relative was the king's uncle, who some years before had been made King of Spain, and was now ruling as Philip V. of that country; and he had renounced all claims to the crown of France when he accepted that of Spain.

After him, the next of kin was the regent, the Duke of Orleans, who was therefore heir presumptive. The regent, however, knew that Philip V. would claim the throne, notwithstanding his vows, and that such a move would involve Europe in warfare; so he hoped that the little king would live and grow up to have children, so that the question would never arise. Such good care was taken of the young king's health that, in spite of a naturally delicate constitution, Louis XV. did live to reign fifty-nine years.

The new master of France, the regent, was a talented but thoroughly unprincipled man, who, wishing to devote most of his time and energy to pleasure, intrusted the government to his former tutor, who was said to be master of all vices. They two canceled Louis XIV.'s will, freed, without question, the prisoners he had locked up in the Bastille and elsewhere, and then took a general survey of the national situation.

The finances were found to be in such a state that Saint-Simon—a nobleman who has left us fascinating Memoirs—seriously advised the regent to pronounce the state bankrupt; that is to say, unable to pay its rightful debts. Bad as he was, however, the regent would not consent to this move, although he frankly acknowledged that things had been so mismanaged that if he were a mere subject he should certainly revolt, saying, "The people are goodnatured fools to suffer so long!"

Painting by Bayard.

Garden Festival at Trianon, near Paris.

Still, instead of trying to remedy these evils, the regent and his minister involved France in a short war with Spain, which added still more to the public debt. Then the regent allowed matters to drift on, while he spent most of his time in the Palais Royal in Paris, reveling with men so wicked that he often said they deserved to be treated like criminals and broken on the wheel *(roues)*. Days and nights were thus spent in orgies of gambling, drunkenness, and other vices.

Such being the case, no one could have an exalted opinion of the regent, to whom a lady once contemptuously said, "God, after having formed man, took the mud which was left, and out of that fashioned the souls of princes and footmen!" Although the regent's sway lasted only eight years, his example did France untold harm, for too many of the nobles eagerly followed in his footsteps, and the people lost all respect for those whom they had hitherto been taught to regard as their superiors.

The regent is also to blame for not having given Louis XV. a good education, and for surrounding him with base flatterers who were anxious only to make him realize his own importance. One tutor, leading him to the palace window, once pointed out the fine gardens and the people assembled to greet him, saying, "Behold, Sire, all this people, all that you see, is yours!"

As the plain truth, if disagreeable, was never told him, Louis XV. naturally had a queer conception of things. Once, for instance, on hearing some mention of a ruler's death, he asked in great surprise, "What! do you mean to say that *kings* die?" Whereupon his embarrassed tutor stammered, "Your Majesty, ...yes...sometimes!" With such an education, and amidst such surroundings, it is no wonder that Louis XV. turned out to be a very bad king, like so many others of his time, and was selfish and unprincipled.

In 1717, when only seven years old, Louis XV. received a visit from Peter the Great of Russia, who, seeing a delicate little boy come slowly down the great staircase to greet him, picked the child up, kissed him on both cheeks, and then carried him upstairs, to the great scandal of the assembled court, which had been trained for two generations in a stately and formal etiquette.

It was in the same year that John Law, a Scotchman, proposed to the regent a scheme for bettering the trade and finances of the country by establishing a new kind of bank. This plan, if carried out exactly as John Law at first intended, would have been all right, as has been demonstrated in many countries. The regent, who was very clever, saw its advantages and therefore allowed John Law to open his bank in Paris. Until then, the only kind of money was specie (gold, silver, and copper), and though there were some bankers in Paris, there were no good savings banks or safe-deposit vaults; so many people kept their funds under lock and key in their own houses. Even small fortunes thus proved both bulky and troublesome, all the more because people were sorely afraid of being robbed, as so many poor were out of work and in a desperate condition.

Law's scheme was to issue paper money and lend it at interest, keeping on hand sufficient gold or silver to redeem each paper bill on demand. He knew that many people would keep on using the paper money in business, instead of getting the coin for it. Indeed, many people who had gold or silver were only too glad to exchange it for paper, which was so much easier to carry or to conceal. Thus, before long, paper money was current everywhere, and Law's bank did a thriving business. On perceiving this fact, the regent declared that the bank should belong to the state, and, as soon as this transfer had been made, insisted that more paper money be issued, the crown lands serving this time as guarantee, as there was no more gold or silver to be had.

Meanwhile, Law had organized the "Mississippi Company," to which was given entire ownership of the vast French colony, Louisiana, in the Mississippi valley, besides a monopoly of the trade with other colonies. It was believed that there would be found rich gold mines in the Mississippi country, so the shares of this company were bought by many people. Next, the company secured all the tax-farming business in France, which was known to be very profitable.

Hitherto, the tax collecting had been done by many different men known as farmers-general, each having charge of a stated district. A farmer-general did not merely collect money for the state, as tax collectors do now; instead, he *bought* the right to collect and *keep* the taxes, having been told something like this: "You see, this district is assessed $100,000, but some of the people can't pay, and a few won't pay promptly. If you will give the state say $75,000 cash, you shall have the right to collect these taxes, and if you are clever about it, you can easily make about $25,000." While honest farmers-general were content to make only the amount thus agreed upon, there were, I am sorry to say, others who increased the taxes and wrung as much money as they could out of the poor people without being punished for it.

Law's company next lent the government, at interest, vast sums in paper money, with which to pay the public debt. Expeditions were sent out to find mines in Louisiana, and people believed that their gold would soon flood France. Shares of the company, selling at first for $100, were soon resold for twenty times as much, and as there always are people anxious to get rich without doing any work in exchange, throngs came to the bank to buy as many shares as they could afford. In fact, such was the demand for shares that they actually could not be printed fast enough!

At the end of three years,—during which some people who had hitherto been poor, had been living like the rich,—the crash suddenly came. The gold mines in the colonies, which were to supply the coin to redeem the paper money and shares, had not been found as yet, so the printed paper suddenly became worthless! A rhyme of the day thus describes the adventures of a shareholder:—

> Monday, I bought shares;
> Tuesday, I was a millionaire;
> Wednesday, I set up an establishment;
> Thursday, I purchased a carriage;

Friday, I went to a ball;
And Saturday . . . to the poorhouse!

Lundi, j'achetai des actions;
  Mardi, je gagnai des millions;
  Mercredi, j'arrangeai anon minage;
  Jeudi, je fit-is Iquifiage;
  Vendredi, je m'enfus au bal;
  Et samedi . . . .a l'hopital!

When the fine scheme of John Law and the regent thus suddenly collapsed, the poor Scotchman barely saved his life by flight, leaving thousands of victims to realize that instead of being better off, as they had so fondly imagined, they were much poorer than before—which, you know, is the invariable result of such disastrous gambling fevers.

While there were, as we have seen, some very bad people in France, there were also fortunately many good ones. When a terrible plague broke out in Marseilles, carrying off eighty-five thousand people, Bishop Belzunce and his clerical staff worked night and day, displaying such self-sacrifice and heroism that the memory of their noble conduct still serves as an inspiration to their fellow-countrymen.

War of the Austrian Succession

The king had barely been proclaimed of age at thirteen, when the wicked regent was stricken with apoplexy. As Louis XV. could not yet take charge of affairs, they were entrusted to the Duke of Bourbon,—a distant relative,— who selected Fleury as his minister. They founded the French Exchange *(Bourse)*, and before long decided that it would be well for the young king to marry as soon as possible so as to have an heir. Louis had been betrothed to a little Spanish princess, who was being educated in France, and upon whom he is said to have bestowed a wonderful doll, worth $5000. But as it would take this child years to grow up, it was decided to send her home and marry the king to Marie, daughter of a dethroned King of Poland (Stanislas Leszczynski), although the lady was seven years older than Louis XV.

The future Queen of France was then living modestly with her parents in a small town of Germany, little dreaming of the exalted position awaiting her. But one day the proud father burst into the room where the princess and her mother were busily sewing, crying out rapturously, "Let us get down on our knees and thank God!" When Marie thereupon wonderingly inquired whether he had been recalled to Poland, he replied, "Better still, you are to be Queen of France!"

Princess Marie married Louis XV. in 1726, and showed her kind heart by immediately distributing among her friends and ladies-in-waiting the sum of money which her royal spouse sent her as a wedding gift *(corbeille)*. Her delight was expressed in the simple exclamation, "Ah! this is the first time in my life that I have been able to make presents!" Louis's queen was good, amiable, gentle, and generous as long as she lived, but never had much influence over her husband, who neglected and insulted her. She was always a devoted mother to the many daughters whom her husband scorned at first, and called by numbers (Madam the First, Madam the Second, etc.), as well as to the long-desired son, next to the youngest in the royal nursery.

The same year that the king married, he craftily got rid of his minister, the Duke of Bourbon, by exiling him, and pretended thereafter to govern the country himself, although all he did was to sit in the council room, playing with a pet cat, while Fleury did the real work of ruling France for seventeen years.

When the ruling King of Poland died and an election took place to decide upon his successor, the father of Queen Marie secured so many votes that he thought it wise to attempt to recover his lost scepter. Louis XV. felt in honor bound to support his father-in-law's claims, and thus France became involved in the War of the Polish Succession (1733-1738). But after the French had won two battles in Italy over the allies of the rival candidate, a treaty was signed, which provided that the French queen's father should have Lorraine instead of Poland, and should leave that province to France at his death. Thus Lorraine became part of France in 1766 and remained French until 1871, when, as we shall see, it was seized by the Prussians.

Peace had not lasted very long, when another war broke out which was to involve all Europe, as well as some of the colonies. This is what is known in Europe as the War of the Austrian Succession, and in United States history as King George's War. By rights there should have been no war at all, for the late Emperor had made all neighboring kings swear not to molest his only daughter, Maria Theresa, whom he appointed, by Pragmatic Sanction (special law) and in his will, sole heir to the Austrian dominions.

But as soon as this Emperor was dead, five different claimants for the Austrian lands arose, and in the conflict which resulted (1741-1748), France, Bavaria, Prussia, and Spain fought against Austria, England, Holland, and Russia. One of the serious engagements was at Dettingen (1743), where George II. of England commanded in person and defeated the French.

The next year, a great sensation was caused in France by the king's severe illness at Metz. In Paris six thousand masses were said at the great church of Notre Dame for his recovery, and when the news finally arrived that he was out of danger, his loyal people were beside themselves with joy. On hearing that they were calling him "Louis the Well-Beloved," the king was so touched that he remorsefully cried, "What have I done to deserve such love?" But whereas Louis XV. seemed truly penitent when near to death, he no sooner recovered his health than he fell back into all his self-indulgent ways.

15

After the Battle of Fontenoy.
(Officers Reporting Victory to the King of France.)

Both the king and the Dauphin ("the Dauphin" was always the title of the king's eldest son, heir to the throne) were present at the battle of Fontenoy, when the English cried, "Gentlemen of the French Guard, fire first." "Fire yourselves, gentlemen of England; we never fire first! retorted the Frenchmen, whose general had told them that those who began the fight were invariably beaten. Although this general (Marshal de Saxe) was very ill at the time, he nevertheless won a brilliant victory, over which there was great rejoicing. This triumph was followed by others, and then the war was ended by the treaty of Aix-la-Chapelle (1748). The King of France, having haughtily declared that "he would treat like a king and not like a merchant," retained none of his conquests; besides, he

Madame de Pompadour

consented to banish the Stuart princes from France,—the refuge of their family ever since the Revolution of 1688 in England).

Shortly after the treaty of Aix-la-Chapelle had been signed, when France was just beginning to enjoy an eight-year period of peace, Louis XV. fell under the spell of the Marquise de Pompadour, a court lady whose original mode of dressing her hair proved fashionable in her day, and has since been revived. Such was the influence of this designing woman, that from 1748 to 1764 she was practically regent of France, appointing ministers and generals according to her fancy, making the king give her one fourth of the public money every year for private expenses, and setting a most pernicious example to both court and nation.

Had she been a good and conscientious woman, Madame de Pompadour was certainly clever enough to have done wonders, but she was really base, and so fickle that France had no less than twenty-five ministers of her choosing in eight years (1755-1763). She worked hard, however, to charm the worthless king and to retain his favor, for she knew how selfish he was, and how easily she might be supplanted and forgotten. This is proved by the remark she once made, "If the king found some one else with whom he could talk about his hunting and his affairs, at the end of three days he would not know the difference if I were gone."

The Misgovernment of Louis XV

Many of the ministers throughout Louis XV.'s reign were very unscrupulous, making much money to line their own pockets by selling blank warrants *(lettres de cachet)*. These warrants,—of which you will hear a great deal,—signed and sealed in the king's name, ordered the arrest and imprisonment in the Bastille or any other state's prison, of the person whose name was to be written on a line, purposely left blank.

The purchaser of such a blank warrant could fill it out whenever he chose, and forward it secretly to the police. Thereupon, the person whose name it bore was seized and locked up instantly, without knowing what for and without being granted any form of trial. Any one who had an enemy, or bore a secret grudge, could purchase such a warrant, and thus get rid of the person who was in his way. We are told that Madame de Pompadour, for instance, actually sent a man to prison for thirty-five years, merely because he had written a mocking rhyme about her!

As one of Louis XV.'s ministers sold no less than 50,000 of these blank warrants, and as over 150,000 were issued during his reign, you can imagine how many—probably innocent—persons were condemned to untold misery in this way. If you wish to learn the sad experience of one of these victims, you will find it in the interesting *Tale of Two Cities* by Charles Dickens.

The king, whose duty it was to remedy such abuses, was instead amusing himself in many wicked and silly ways. Besides the hunt, his chief pastime was making tarts and candy, and he prided himself far more upon the dexterity with which he could chip off the top of a soft-boiled egg, than upon anything else. In fact, such was his puerile vanity, and such the silliness of the base courtiers whom he gathered around him, that when Louis chipped an egg at breakfast, they always cried, "Long live the king!" as heartily as if he had performed some heroic deed.

Meantime, many of the people, sinking under the burdens placed upon them by tax collectors and nobles, were literally starving. Their sufferings and burdens seemed more intolerable than ever before, because they were now sufficiently well informed to realize how selfish and wicked this king was, and how much money was wasted in buying him royal mantles embroidered with gold and weighing one hundred and eighty pounds, besides rich jewels and other luxuries for his favorites. In fact, the king—once called the Well-Beloved—was now secretly hated, and some people were so convinced of his infamy and heartlessness, that they actually made an ogre of him, relating with bated breath "that he bathed in the blood of little children" to keep a good complexion!

Such being the state of affairs, you will not be surprised to learn that an attempt was made to murder Louis XV. (1757). The would-be murderer, caught in the very act, and brought before the king, solemnly warned him, saying, "If you do not take the part of your people, you, the Dauphin and many others will perish before many years." But this warning fell upon deaf ears, and the execution of this man was fully as cruel as that of the assassin of Henry IV., for he was first tortured, then partly hanged, and finally torn to pieces.

With such an example as the king's in high places, you can readily imagine that many of the nobles also were leading selfish, useless, and wicked lives. But fortunately there were still many good, honorable people left, such as the aristocrat who once, when taunted for his blameless life, answered haughtily, I possess all kinds of courage except that which can brave shame."

The French people—the commoners—resented their misgovernment more and more fiercely, for they had learned many things of late years, and were daily discovering more. The progress of literature in the "Age of Louis XIV." was almost, if not quite, equaled by the advance made in science under Louis XV. In fact, it has been said that "a revolution of ink" took place in this reign, when Diderot published the first encyclopedia, Linnaeus classified plants, Buffon wrote a natural history, and other scientists also did valuable work.

The three greatest literary men of this time were Montesquieu, Voltaire, and Rousseau,—names which you will often hear. Montesquieu is noted for his criticisms of society and his historical studies; Voltaire for his brilliant work in both prose and poetry; and Rousseau for his eloquent novels and fine educational theories. But, while preaching beautifully on the duties of parents to their children, Rousseau used to drop his own in the cradle then placed at the door of all foundling asylums, simply because he did not want to have the trouble of bringing them up! Still, notwithstanding his own bad morals and example, Rousseau gave excellent advice, and his works had a tremendous influence in France for many years, although now they are principally admired for their beauty of style.

The Seven Years' War—known in United States history as the French and Indian War—lasted from 1756 till 1763. It was occasioned by England's desire to monopolize all the ocean trade, and by Austria's desire to recover territory lost to Prussia during the War of the Austrian Succession. In this conflict, France, Saxony, Austria, and Russia fought against Prussia and England, and the war raged not only in Europe, but also in America and in India, where the French had gradually been acquiring an empire, thanks to intrepid explorers and heroic soldiers. The most interesting part of this war took place in Canada, but there was also much fighting in Europe, where the French won several minor battles and lost several important ones (Rossbach, Crefeld, and Minden).

The Seven Years' War, concluded by the treaty of Paris (1763), left France shorn of the greater part of her colonial possessions, Canada and India passing into the hands of the English, who have retained their hold upon them ever since.

Painting by Cain.

Pajou making a Bust of Madame du Barry.

This war is also known as the "War of Madame de Pompadour," because she chose most of the generals who carried it on. When she perceived that

19

the king seemed distressed after one of the defeats, she comforted him, until he could cheerily repeat his favorite maxim, "Things will last my day," to which she recklessly added, "After us, the deluge!" You see, she was so very selfish that anything which did not touch her closely seemed of no moment at all.

It was in the course of the Seven Years' War that the "Family Compact" was first made by the minister Choiseul, whereby the Bourbon rulers of France, Spain, and parts of Italy promised to uphold one another, the enemy of one country being henceforth considered a foe of all.

Two years after the war was ended, Louis XV. lost his son, the Dauphin, a very promising young man, who left three sons, all of whom were to reign over France in turn (Louis XVI., Louis XVIII., and Charles X.). The same year, the king's favorite, Madame de Pompadour, also passed away; and the cold-blooded monarch, when he saw rain falling on the day of her funeral, calmly remarked, "The Marquise will not have good weather for her journey." These were his only words of sympathy for a woman for whom he had spent many, many millions of the state money!

But one favorite being gone was only the signal for the appearance of another. The weak and vicious Louis XV. now became the tool of a woman of common birth, who was known as Madame du Barry. She was even more extravagant than Madame de Pompadour, encouraged the king in his evil ways, ran the state ever deeper into debt, and scandalized all decent people by her manners and language. She swore openly, talked the lowest kind of slang to induce the king to smile, and encouraged the ministers to consider the people solely "as a sponge to be squeezed."

Marriage of Marie Antoinette

The States-General had not been called to meet since 1614, so the people could make their grievances known only by means of petitions,—which were generally disregarded,—or through the parliaments, assemblies of judges and lawyers in some of the great cities. The Parliament of Paris becoming troublesome on account of its repeated demands for redress of grievances, the king was glad to heed the warning given by Madame du Barry when he was once gazing at the portrait of the unfortunate Charles I. of England. Said she: "Look, France! there is a king whose head was cut off because he was indulgent to his Parliament. Go, now, and be indulgent to yours!" Owing to this taunt, Louis XV. exiled seven hundred members of parliament (1771) before calling a new assembly, which was composed of men carefully select-ed by the chancellor Maupeou, and was hence derisively called "Maupeou's Parliament."

But the grievances continued, the court expenditures increased, and the misery of the poor became so intense that we are told more men died of hunger in one year than were slain in the course of all Louis XIV.'s wars! This sad state of affairs was well known to the king, who paid no more heed to it than to the funeral he once met, when, having inquired of what disease the man had died, and having been curtly told, "Hunger!" he merely shrugged his shoulders and passed on.

The Jesuits—members of the Society of Jesus, founded by Loyola—had done much in France, as in other countries, to stamp out Protestantism and build up the Roman Catholic Church. But in the exercise of their great influence through preaching and teaching and as a political force in the affairs of state, the Jesuits soon became the objects of great dislike on the part of many—notably the writer Pascal. When they also incurred the dislike of the king, they were banished from France, as they had already been driven from some other European countries.

To gain riches for himself, Louis XV. took part in a disgraceful speculation to raise the price of wheat. This still further intensified the sufferings of the poor, upon whom fell the heaviest burdens of taxation.

Louis XV., who fully believed that "the king is master, and necessity justifies everything," required so much money for his court and his pleasures that taxes were nearly doubled during his reign. His nobles also spent vast amounts, being very particular about their clothes, lace ruffles, silk stockings, and jewelry. Those who paid most attention to these trifles were, in those days, called "macaroni," a name with which Americans are familiar because it occurs in "Yankee Doodle." As such courtiers liked to have their pictures painted, they often patronized such artists as Mignard and Boucher, who were so fond of finery that even their shepherds are clad in silks and lead snow-white sheep by blue or pink ribbons! Thus, you see, everything was artificial, and nothing plain and real.

The minister (Choiseul) who incurred the people's hatred by raising the taxes has the credit of restoring the navy of France, and of negotiating (1770) a marriage between the king's grandson—the new Dauphin—and Marie Antoinette, a daughter of Maria Theresa, the heroine of the War of the Austrian Succession.

When Marie Antoinette came to France, a merry girl of fifteen, to be married to a heavy, awkward, yet good-natured lad of sixteen, she found a stiff court, ruled by the etiquette which had been in practice for about one hundred years, and which was severely enforced by a mistress of ceremonies whom Marie Antoinette disrespectfully called Madam Etiquette." All the formality now surrounding her proved intensely tiresome to a lively young girl, who, besides, felt the utmost contempt for Madame du Barry,—the most important person in the palace,—for the old king was merely her puppet. You will see that scorn for long-established customs, although natural enough, was to do Marie Antoinette much harm in time.

Besides a Dauphiness,—who was to be one of the most famous and unfortunate queens of France,—the country acquired during Louis XV.'s reign not only the province of Lorraine, but also the island of Corsica. This island was acquired from Genoa only a few months before the birth of Napoleon Bonaparte (Aug. 15, 1769), who thus by accident born a Frenchman—was for many years to make history for Europe.

During Louis XV.'s reign, also,—thanks to the efforts of patriotic citizens,—military, engineering, and medical schools were founded; the first asylum for deaf-mutes was instituted; a few fine roads were built; the porcelain factory of Sevres was established; the Pantheon was erected; street lamps were installed; and the first art exhibition was opened to the public.

But in 1774 this long reign came to an end. Louis. XV., who was a loathsome man, suddenly caught a loathsome disease, and died of smallpox. The terrible harvest he had so guiltily sown was left to be reaped by his innocent grandson, Louis XVI.

Beginning of Louis XVI.'s Reign

While Louis XV. was slowly breathing his last, his grandson and heir, Louis XVI.,—then only twenty years old,—was waiting with his young wife, Marie Antoinette, for news of his death. A candle, burning in the king's window, was to be quenched as a signal when the end actually occurred, and as its light went out the young couple fell on their knees together, crying: "Oh, God, guide us and protect us! We are too young to reign!"

But only a moment was granted them in which to ask divine help for the great task awaiting them; for all the courtiers were already racing along the palace corridors, "making a noise like thunder," each anxious to be first to hail the new sovereign by name and do him homage.

The present king was a contrast to the last in every respect, for he was pious, virtuous, slow in motion and mind, and very anxious to do his duty so as to relieve the people, whom he sincerely pitied. Louis XVI. was also very modest. Even when he was a little boy, if some one praised him, he was wont to say, "You surely, mean my brother, for he is the clever boy!" His brothers were, indeed, far more clever than he, but unfortunately they were not nearly so good, for they thought only of their own advantage, and gave the slow-witted king very bad advice at times.

Although Louis really meant to do all that was right and proper, he had not been well trained for his position, and had, besides, grown up with the worst of models in the court ever before his eyes. He therefore did not know exactly where to begin or what to do, but set a good example in morals to court and people, dismissed the wicked persons who had had so much influence over his grandfather, and placed the government in the hands of good ministers, among whom we can name Turgot and Malesherbes.

Everybody now hoped great things for the country, for one morning an inscription was found upon the pedestal of Henry IV.'s statue to the effect that he had come to life again in Louis XVI. The next day, however, an addition was made to it, purporting that the good tidings would be believed only when every citizen had a chicken in his pot,—showing that mere promises would no longer satisfy the nation.

Dairy in the Little Trianon.

In his leisure moments, when not busy with affairs of state, Louis amused himself with map making—for geography was one of his hobbies; taking lessons from a locksmith in the art of making keys and locks; and spending, besides, much time in hunting. For his young wife's amusement, he bestowed upon her the Little Trianon, a miniature palace with grounds of its own in the park of Versailles. There the queen laid out an English garden, and built a tiny model village, in which she, her husband, and the court could play at being rustics. Her chief delight was to make butter and cheese in her dainty dairy, while her husband, who prided himself upon his great strength, often acted the part of miller, carrying heavy sacks of grain to the mill to be ground into flour for his wife's bread and cakes! Another favorite pastime consisted in picnics, and once, when Marie Antoinette was thrown by a sportive donkey, she sat on the grass laughing merrily, and told the courtiers, who rushed up to help her remount: "Go get the mistress of ceremonies. She will tell you what etiquette prescribes when a Queen of France cannot manage to stay on her donkey!"

The simple occupations the court now affected would have been harmless, had not important duties been waiting, which should have occupied all the time of both the king and the queen of such a great country. But the poor young people—one nineteen, the other twenty years old—did not know any better, and in time had to pay not only for their own innocent shortcomings, but for the awful sins of their predecessors as well.

Meantime, every one was watching them closely, for it was whispered at court that two bad omens heralded an unlucky reign. The first was that, when the people assembled near the Tuileries—an old palace in Paris—to see fireworks set off in honor of their wedding, a misdirected rocket had occasioned a stampede, which caused the death of many persons. The second bad sign was that at the coronation the king complained of his crown, saying: "How heavy it is! It hurts me!" This was enough for superstitious people, and when the crown indeed became too heavy for this blameless but simple-minded ruler, many people declared they had long foreseen what would come to pass!

It was said that "under Louis XIV. no one dared speak, and under Louis XV. people spoke only with bated breath," but no one was at all afraid of good-natured Louis XVI., and therefore "everybody spoke aloud." Because the king hesitated, not knowing what to do, everybody felt called upon to give him good advice. His clever brother, called Monsieur, the young queen, and the courtiers all claimed his ear in turn. Like many dull people, Louis was always inclined to believe the last speaker, and therefore often changed his mind. One of his brothers accurately described the situation to a minister by saying, "When you can make a pyramid of a number of oiled ivory balls, you may do something with the king!"

Turgot's Ministry

The minister Turgot had governed one French province well for many years, and had prevented the people there from suffering from hunger like the rest of the nation, by planting potatoes. Until then, root crops (turnips, beets, carrots, and potatoes) had been neglected in France, so at first people distrusted the new food, believing it would produce terrible diseases. But when they saw that Turgot himself ate potatoes, and when the king wore potato blossoms in his buttonhole, popular opinion began to change.

There is, besides, another famous story of how people were induced to raise potatoes. It is said that Turgot or another man had a sandy stretch planted with them, and carefully guarded the growing crop, but artfully let it become noised abroad that it was precious beyond price! Of course, such secrecy and care aroused popular curiosity, and it was generally believed that if potatoes had to be guarded so closely, they must be extra good. Very soon, therefore, a few were stolen and stealthily planted, and before long the new food became popular everywhere.

When Turgot took charge of the affairs of France, he found them in a desperate condition. The debt was larger than ever before, the revenues were in confusion, and expenses were greater than income. Still, Turgot was hopeful of bringing order out of chaos in time, if the king would only uphold him. This Louis XVI. faithfully promised to do, knowing that Turgot was capable and had good intentions, for he often said, "There is no one save Turgot and me who love the people!"

As Turgot was honest, he did not declare the state bankrupt; on the contrary, he proposed to cut down expenses, and to ease the burdens of taxation. His policy was, "No bankruptcy, no increase of taxes, no loans." He also encouraged his master in effecting such reforms as restoring the Parliament of Paris, and freeing those who had been unjustly imprisoned. The result was that the people were soon really better off than they had been for more than a hundred years past; but unfortunately they had suffered so much that their patience was almost exhausted, and gradual improvement failed to satisfy men who wanted everything at once.

Turgot kept on working hard to improve conditions for two years, but as the king was always interfering, by yielding first to this adviser and then to that, the minister finally gave up all hope of doing much good. On leaving, he said, "All I desire, Sire, is that you may always be able to believe that I was shortsighted and that I pointed out to you fanciful dangers!" Later on he also wrote to the master whose downfall he was not to live long enough to witness, "Do not forget, Sire, that it was weakness which put the head of Charles I. of England on the block; that it was weakness which produced the League under Henry III. and which made slaves of Louis XIII. and of the present King of Portugal; it was weakness also which caused all the misfortunes of the late reign."

In spite of these solemn warnings, Louis continued weak; he could not help it. As we shall see, it was his weakness and his pernicious habit of putting things off which caused the outbreak of the terrible French Revolution.

Louis's other great minister, Malesherbe, like Turgot, also found difficulties too great to contend with, and when he handed in his resignation, his master exclaimed with an envious sigh, "You are very lucky, for you can give up your job!" This feeling became more intense as time went on, for when another minister (Vergennes) died in 1787, the king said, gazing down into his tomb, "Oh, how happy I should be if I were only lying beside you in that grave!"

The American Revolution

As Marie Antoinette had no babies to take care of during the first eight years of her marriage, she had plenty of time to amuse herself with her dairy village; to act in plays with the Count of Artois, her youngest brother-in-law; to study the music of Mozart, Gluck, and Gretry, whose operas she loved; and even to meddle in government affairs. But in 1778 her first child (Marie Therese Charlotte), who was to be known as Madam Royal, came to enliven the palace of Versailles, so the queen devoted herself to the care and education of this little one, instead of giving her up to governesses and attendants, as had hitherto been the custom at court. From that time on Marie Antoinette ceased to be frivolous, and proved the best of mothers, not only to this little girl, but to three other children who came later on.

It was shortly after Louis XVI.'s reign began that war broke out between England and her American colonies (1775). As you have doubtless read much about that war in other books, you will now be especially interested in the part which France took in the struggle. Twelve years before, as you remember, France had been obliged to give Canada to England (1763), and the French still felt sore about their loss. When Benjamin Franklin came to Paris, therefore, in search of aid for the rebellious Thirteen Colonies, he was warmly welcomed, not only because he was already favorably known on account of his marvelous scientific discoveries, but also because he represented a people who were trying to secure the liberty about which recent writers had said so much.

Painting by Jolly.

A French Reception in Honor of Benjamin Franklin.

While Louis XVI. was hesitating whether or not to help the Thirteen Colonies, Lafayette, a young French nobleman, left his wife, freighted a vessel himself, and, escaping secretly from France, sailed across the ocean to offer his services to General Washington. But, knowing that to aid the Americans openly would involve war with England, Louis XVI. could not at first be induced to do anything except to supply money; still, in 1778, he at last signed a commercial treaty with the United States at Versailles. Thus France, you see, was the first European power to recognize the new nation.

As Louis had foreseen, this move resulted in war with England, which, being far too busy elsewhere to fight the French on land, merely challenged their men-of-war in naval duels. As the French took the utmost interest in the conflict between England and her colonies, they made a lion of Franklin, who remained in their midst about nine years, spending pleasant hours with such famous scientists as Mesmer(the man whose discoveries in animal magnetism received the name of Mesmerism), and Montgolfier, whose first balloon was tried before the court of Versailles in 1783. Whenever people asked Franklin how the American Revolution was getting on, he used to say,—nodding his head confidently, for his French was imperfect,—"Ca ira!". This laconic expression, which can be translated, "That will be all right!" so amused everybody that it was generally adopted, and became at last the rallying cry of the French Revolution, as well as the refrain of a popular song.

Now, as you know, Franklin's prophetic words came true; things did go all right for the United States. But after their independence had been duly recognized by the treaty of Paris (1783), France discovered that she had run herself still further into debt by the help she had given the Americans. Besides, the young men who had gone across the Atlantic to lend the Revolutionary army aid, came back full of their adventures, wild with admiration for the American people, and anxious to instill into the minds and hearts of their countrymen the republican ideas they had recently absorbed.

During part of this time, the finances of France had been in the hands of a Swiss banker, Necker, who tried to reduce expenses in every way, but only succeeded in angering everybody by his constant talk of economy. His successor, Calonne, believed in acting very differently, for whenever the king and queen doubtfully inquired whether anything could be done, he used to reassure them by saying, "If it is possible, it is already done; if it is not possible, it will be done." But, so as to *do* things, Calonne recklessly borrowed right and left, thus adding $100,000,000 to the state debt, before making place for Brienne, who found it necessary to borrow still more.

It was about this time that the idyllic story of *Paul and Virginia* by Bernardin de St. Pierre first appeared (1788), and that plays by Beaumarchais, criticizing the aristocracy, began to become popular, although when they first came out they, encountered the king's censure. The most famous artists of the day, were Vernet for landscapes and marines, Greuze for fancy *(genre)* subjects, and Madame Lebrun, to whom we owe the best pictures of the royal family, as well as charming studies of herself and her child.

The Queen's Necklace

The most thrilling event in the court life of this period was the affair of the Diamond Necklace (1784), which you must hear in detail, as it had a fatal influence later on. King Louis XV. had ordered from the court jeweler a $450,000 necklace of diamonds for Madame du Barry; but as he died before it was ready, the half-finished necklace remained on the jeweler's hands. Having spent large sums to get and match the stones, this man felt that he would be ruined if he could not dispose of the completed necklace, so he now offered it to Marie Antoinette. But, having two children,—a daughter and son,—she was inclined to be more serious and saving than she had been. As she would not do anything more than to praise his wares, the jeweler next applied to the king, who, devoted as he was, immediately offered to present the wonderful necklace to his wife.

But Marie Antoinette now restrained her husband, saying she had jewels enough, and that the money would be far better employed in adding a ship or two to his navy, which sensible advice Louis XVI. gladly took. The jeweler now went from court to court, hawking his necklace, but finding no one with money enough to spare to buy so costly a bauble. In his despair he finally returned to the French queen, it is said, and fell at her feet, beseeching her with tears to buy his wares, and thus save him from ruin! This theatrical scene greatly annoyed Marie Antoinette, who, deeming the man crazy, sent him away as soon as possible.

There was then at court a French nobleman, Cardinal de Rohan, who was anxious to regain the queen's favor, which he had forfeited by a wicked life and by wanton slanders he had spread regarding her. Still, the royal couple were too kind-hearted to resent anything very long, so after a few years' banishment, the cardinal was allowed to return to court, where a fashionable astrologer (Cagliostro) had, it seems, predicted that all would go as the cardinal wished. In some obscure position at Versailles, at that time, there was also an adventuress named Madame de la Motte. This woman wanted money badly, and often thought how lucky she would be if she could only get hold of the wonderful diamond necklace. Being as clever as unprincipled, she soon hit upon a plan to secure it.

Madame de la Motte and the astrologer persuaded the cardinal that the queen was anxious to have the diamonds, and would be most grateful to any one who would arrange so that she could purchase them without telling the king. Nobody now knows whether the cardinal was the dupe of these two clever schemers, or whether he was a third party in their dishonest plans. However that may be, Cardinal de Rohan soon went to the jeweler, and declared that the queen wished him to buy the necklace in her name, promising that the full price should be paid within a year and a half by installments.

This was welcome news for the despairing jeweler; still, he was too shrewd to give up his necklace until he had the queen's written promise. Cardinal de Rohan, therefore, undertook to get it, and actually came back a few days later with a paper signed "Marie Antoinette de France." Now, both merchant and cardinal should have known that it was only the *children* of French kings who added "de France" to their signatures, yet both men overlooked this forgery, and necklace and paper changed hands.

Meantime, Cardinal de Rohan had been deluded by Madame de la Motte into believing that the queen herself had stolen down into the garden one moonlight night, and had allowed him to kiss her hand. But in reality it was a young actress who had come there, after being coached to personate the queen. The cardinal, of course, expected to deliver the necklace to Marie Antoinette in person, but Madame de la Motte, disguised as a royal footman, took charge of it, reporting that the queen was too ill to see him. Then the adventuress carried the precious necklace off to her own room, where her husband pried the diamonds out of their settings, and secretly sent them to England to be sold.

While these rascals were living in luxury on the proceeds of their theft, the queen continued no more gracious to the cardinal than before, and never appeared in public wearing the necklace. Then, too, the payments were not forthcoming as promised. The jeweler waited impatiently, and one day—being summoned to court by the queen, who wished to buy a wedding present for one of her maids—he ventured to beg her for money, saying he had already written, but had received no reply. Although the queen had received the letter he mentioned, she had thrown it into the fire, thinking the man was crazy, a belief which was strengthened by this strange request for money. Finding himself dismissed without pay, the desperate jeweler now went straight to the king, although it was Sunday morning, and poured out the whole story. Louis XVI. immediately sent for the queen, and then for Cardinal de Rohan, who had just been celebrating mass in the Versailles chapel.

The cardinal at once appeared in the king's study, but when questioned, stammered and contradicted himself so sorely, looking so embarrassed, that Louis kindly bade him go into the next room, and write what he had to say, since he could not speak plainly. There the cardinal wrote an even lamer statement, but before beginning it, he scribbled a note which he handed to one of his servants. According to the instructions thus given, this servant hastened home and burned all the papers contained in a red portfolio. These papers were not only the correspondence in regard to the diamond necklace, but also many proofs of the wicked life the cardinal had hitherto led, which he did not wish any one to see.

On reading the cardinal's written statement, accusing the queen of having a secret understanding with him, the king became so angry that he ordered Rohan's arrest; vowing that he should be tried immediately. But as the cardinal was a priest, the clergy were indignant that he should be arrested in canonical garb; and as he was related to many of the nobles, they, too, were furious to think that one of their number should be treated like a common wrongdoer. Both of these influential classes, therefore, set to work to influence the Parliament so that no unfavorable sentence should be pronounced.

The trial took place; king, queen, and everybody was present. It was proved at the end of six months that the diamonds had passed into the hands of the De la Mottes, and that the paper signed by "Marie Antoinette de France" was a mere forgery. The Parliament was glad to defy the king by finding the cardinal not guilty; but it sentenced Madame de la Motte to be whipped and branded as a thief, and then shut up in prison. The astrologer was banished, the cardinal was sent away from court, and the queen was really acquitted of all knowledge of the affair.

But the wretched De la Motte woman soon made her escape to England, where she began to write pamphlets about the Queen's Necklace, claiming that she and the poor cardinal had been made scapegoats for Marie Antoinette's sins! These pamphlets were scattered far and wide, smuggled into France, and read everywhere, in spite of the king's attempts to suppress them. Now, many people are ready, to believe anything that is printed, and most people say that a wife who makes debts and hides the fact from her husband is dishonest. Poor Marie Antoinette, therefore, was generally considered not only cowardly because she allowed some one else to bear the punishment of her sins, but also wanting in honor and decency, and terribly extravagant, since she purchased high-priced ornaments when her people were starving!

Many of the old court ladies, who disliked her because she made thoughtless fun of their grand manners when she

Marie Antoinette and Her Children

was a merry girl, had always spoken ill of her, declaring she was nothing but a "foreigner," and generally calling her "the Austrian." Now the people in general exclaimed that it was no wonder there was a deficit in the nation's finances, when the queen was extravagant enough to purchase $450,000 worth of diamonds at once; and they dubbed her "Madam Deficit." In fact, such was Marie Antoinette's unpopularity after this affair, that the king no longer dared let her visit Paris, for fear lest she should be insulted in his capital!

Meantime, Louis XVI: continued to relieve the public misery to some small extent by private charities. He chided those who spent money to refurnish his rooms, remarking sadly, "I could have supported thirty families for a year with that sum!" During the cold winters he sent many loads of wood to the poor, and once with innocent pride pointed out his train of sledges to the courtiers when they gleefully exhibited their elegant pleasure vehicles.

The Fall of the Bastille

The heavy taxes collected from the common people (Third Estate) were still far too little to pay the interest on the public debt and the running expenses of the government. Because of the awful want of money, Louis XVI. called a small assembly of notables (1787), hoping to obtain good advice; but the nobles and clergy would not consent to be taxed, and the assembly accomplished nothing. The Parliament of Paris refused to register decrees for new taxes on the people, but was compelled to yield. However, the prime minister Brienne, in proposing an addition to the public debt, promised to convene the States-General, which had not met for one hundred and seventy-five years (since 1614), but for which the people were now clamoring.

Brienne did not intend to keep his promise, but he soon lost his place, which was given again to Necker; and Necker persuaded the king to call the States-General. The call for the election was therefore at last made; and as the king decided that he must remain in Versailles for the hunting, the nobility, clergy, and elected representatives of the Third Estate were summoned to meet there on the 6th of May, 1789.

The opening of the States General was a solemn pageant. King, queen, court, nobles, priests, and citizens (bourgeois)—representing the thirty-two provinces in France—marched in imposing procession to the great hall, where Louis made a brief address, in which he "assured his people of his affection," and urged them to do nothing rash. Then Necker, his minister, read a long speech, in which the States-General were requested, principally, to devise means whereby state finances could be satisfactorily supplied.

When these preliminaries were all over, the members of the assembly, left alone to deliberate, immediately began to quarrel. In olden times there had been only about as many representatives of the Third Estate as of the nobles or of the clergy. But since then the population and importance of the lower class had increased greatly, and thanks to Necker there had now been summoned twice as many commoners as usual, so that they were slightly greater in number than both nobles and clergy combined. Hitherto, it had been customary for the three orders to sit and vote in separate rooms, each order casting one vote, but the Third Estate now demanded that all should meet and vote together in one room.

The king was pestered by deputations, each wanting him to do this or that, while he was distracted by the fatal illness of his eldest son, the Dauphin, who died on the 4th of June. This was the second child to leave the royal nursery, a little sister having died when a year old. Little did people then dream how fortunate the boy was to go thus, and be spared the tortures endured by his poor young brother, who is known as the second Dauphin.

When members of the States-General clamored to see Louis XVI., a few days after his son's death, he despairingly cried, "Shall I then not even be allowed to weep for my child?" But the king could not be granted much leisure to nurse paternal grief, for in spite of his many wise concessions and reforms, the people were now in such a ferment of discontent, that no less than three hundred riots took place in the country within four months' time.

The Tennis Court Oath

Hoping to end the disputes of the three orders, which threatened never to end, Louis XVI. suddenly ordered the hall closed, under some trifling pretext. But, thus shut out, the Third Estate met tumultuously in the Versailles Tennis Court, where, after a lively discussion, they bound themselves, by the famous "Tennis Court Oath," never to separate until they had given a new constitution to France.

Next, the king in person, at a meeting of the States-General, commanded the three orders to retire each to its own room, to sit separately. The nobles and the clergy accordingly went out when the king did, but the Third Estate remained. When again ordered to go, their spokesman, Mirabeau, boldly replied to the royal messenger, "Go and tell your master that we are here by the will of the people, and that we will not go until driven out by bayonets." Louis XIV. could say, "*I* am the state!" but his successor could not, for the voices of the people were now loudly declaring, "*We* are the state!"

Four days later the long dispute was ended as the Third Estate wished, and it was finally settled that the three orders should meet and vote together

(June 27). This agreement was brought about mainly by the pleas of a few members of the nobility, and by many of the clergy, who, knowing how much the people suffered, were anxious to relieve their distress as soon as possible.

The States-General, instead of merely supplying funds as Necker wished, now began to discuss the causes of popular discontent. They discovered that most of the trouble could be ascribed, 1st, to ten successive years of bad harvests; 2nd, to class privileges; 3rd, to various services which the people had to render free of charge to their superiors; and 4th, to the blindness of royalty in not perceiving sooner how times had changed.

Although the king gently explained all the improvements he had already made, nothing would content the States-General save the right to have a voice henceforth in government affairs; the assurance that their assembly should not be disbanded until it had finished its constitutional work, and a formal promise that States-General should henceforth meet at regular intervals. It seemed as if after these claims had been granted, everything might have run on smoothly, had not the news come that Necker had been dismissed, and that the king was collecting troops near Versailles, presumably to awe the people and their representatives.

The Garden of the Palais Royal

When these tidings reached Paris, then a city of 800,000 inhabitants,—many of whom were out of work,—Desmouins, an eloquent young patriot, made a fiery speech in the garden of the Palais Royal, urging the mob to rebel. This speech proved like a spark in a keg of powder, and when Desmou-

33

lins next suggested that the citizens stick green leaves in their caps as a rallying sign, the trees in the garden were stripped in the twinkling of an eye. The excited multitude then marched around the city, carrying a bust of Necker; and after coming to blows with a body of troops, proceeded to plunder the arsenals. Then, fully armed, they rushed madly off to tear down the Bastille, the terrible fortress where so many prisoners had once been confined, and from whose towers cannon could easily destroy the homes where so many of them lived.

Had the Bastille been properly provisioned, it could have held out for many months; but its governor being assured that no one would be injured if he opened the gates, preferred to do so rather than further infuriate the mob. No sooner were the doors opened, than the people swept in to liberate the prisoners. They found seven in all, four of whom were forgers, two insane, and one an unfortunate young man with a tendency to drink, who was kept there out of harm's way at his father's request. The Bastille had already, you see, ceased to be a prison filled with innocent people, arrested by royal warrant and detained there without trial.

The Fall of the Bastille

The mob had been admitted, but the promises made by some of the leaders were utterly disregarded by others, who seized the governor, and, while leading him off to the city hall (Hotel de Ville), suddenly decided to hang him. Street lamps had recently been introduced in Paris; they were swung from great iron brackets, and to be filled or lighted they were hoisted up and down by means of a rope. These iron brackets being strong, and a rope so handy, when the frantic cry suddenly arose, "To the lamp with, him!" *(A la lanterne)*, a host of volunteer hangmen proceeded to dispose of the poor man. The rope, not designed for such an office, repeatedly broke; still, the wretches persevered until their victim's sufferings were at an end. And that terrible cry, thus heard for the first time at the execution of the governor of the Bastille, was to be repeated with alarming frequency in the course of the next few years.

While some of the mob were thus hanging an innocent man, the remainder had already begun to demolish the Bastille, many of the stones of which were used later for the construction of one of the bridges across the Seine (Pont de la Concorde). This fall of the Bastille, July 14, 1789, is considered the Declaration of Independence of the French people, who now celebrate its anniversary just as Americans do their 4th of July.

The news about its capture reached Versailles, about ten miles away, in the middle of the night, and when the king was roused to hear what had been done, he exclaimed in dismay, "Why! this is a revolt!"

"No, Sire," replied his informer gravely, "it is a Revolution!"

This man was right; the terrible French Revolution had begun.

The Mob at Versailles

Feeling that something must be done immediately to pacify the excited Parisians, Louis XVI. announced on the very next day the recall of Necker, and the dismissal of the troops. He also consented to the people's choice of Lafayette as general-in-chief of the National Guards,—the militia of Paris,—and Bailly as mayor of Paris, making them responsible for order in the capital. Then the king, who was no coward physically, drove straight off to Paris, where the mayor received him at the gates, presenting the keys, as usual, with this speech: "Sire, I am bringing to your Majesty the keys of your good city of Paris. They are the same that were presented to Henry IV. He had reconquered his people; now the people have reconquered their king!"

Proceeding to the city hall, the king was next met by Lafayette, who offered him a blue and red badge, the colors of Paris. The king graciously accepted this pledge of amity, suggesting, however, that the white of royalty be placed between them. The combined colors so pleased Lafayette,—already familiar with the American red, white, and blue,—that he exclaimed with enthusiasm, "Sire, this cockade will go around the world!"

But pretty speeches could not stop the ball once set rolling, and when the news sped from mouth to mouth through France that the Parisians had pulled down the Bastille, mobs elsewhere, fired by such an example, began to set fire to castles here and there. Besides, the cry of "Bread! Bread!" was heard on all sides, and many bread riots took place. One official was reported to have said to those who complained they had no bread, "Well, go out then and eat grass!" In a riot he was hanged from a street lamp bracket, then taken down, and his severed head was paraded through the streets with its mouth stuffed full of hay. Many others were summarily disposed of in this way, yet so fickle is a mob that we are told one man saved his life by dryly retorting, when they proposed to hang him up instead of the, lamp, "Well, will you see any better when you have done so?"

The report of murders, burning castles, and uncontrolled mobs proved more than the nerves of some aristocrats could endure, so they hastily packed up and left the country, fully intending to return as soon as all was safe. Because these nobles emigrated, or left their native country, they were generally known as "the émigrés". Among the first to go was the younger brother of the king, who hastened to put his precious head in safety, leaving his elders to manage as best they could. At first all tidings of such departures were hailed with delight, the people crying, "So much the better; France is being purged!" But later on the nation resented the flight of its aristocratic class, against which it nursed a bitter grudge.

There were still, however, many truly patriotic noblemen in France, who, seeing the people were angry because the nobles had "privileges,"—paid no direct taxes, paid no wages for a certain amount of labor from the peasants, etc.,—and hoping to prevent a general uprising of the peasants, volunteered to give up all their privileges and feudal rights. The States-General—known since the Tennis Court Oath as the National Assembly—accepted their offers, and issued, besides, many decrees in favor of the people, announcing among other things that thereafter all citizens should have the right to profess any religion they pleased in France, where "there was now but one land, one nation, one family, and one title—that of French citizen."

Just as it began to look as if things would quiet down, the people of Paris—who were nearly starving—became exasperated at news that a grand banquet had been given to a regiment at Versailles. When the king, queen, and Dauphin had appeared there for a moment, it was said, they were greeted by enthusiastic cries of, "Long live their Majesties!" and white cockades—the royal colors—were substituted for the red, white, and blue, which were basely trampled under foot.

Such a report proved enough to make the caldron boil madly again. One woman, seizing a drum, began to beat it loudly, proclaiming that all the women ought to march to Versailles to demand bread for themselves and their starving families. In less time than one would think possible, nine thousand women of the lowest class in the city set out for Versailles, shouting, "Bread! Bread!" every step of the way. Many men joined them. Lafayette, who was responsible for order in the city, after vainly trying to stop this mob, summoned his troops to follow, so as to see that no harm would ensue; but his movements proved so leisurely that the rabble reached Versailles before he did.

In front of the royal palace, the cries of this mob rose shriller and shriller, until the king came out to pacify them, promising even to return with them to Paris on the morrow. Then the mob began to clamor for the queen, but as she was known to be misjudged and disliked, king and ministers tried to prevent her from responding to these calls. Brave Marie Antoinette, however, taking a child in each hand, stepped quietly out on a balcony, in full view of the throng.

Silence received her, then all at once the yell arose:

"No children! No children!" Still without a tremor, Marie Antoinette led the children in, and came out again, alone, expecting to be stoned to death, but showing no fear. It was this dauntless courage that saved her, for the people stood paralyzed by astonishment, until Lafayette, who had just arrived, stepped out on the balcony, and in full view of the crowd respectfully kissed the royal hand. Then a sudden revulsion took place, cheers arose, and the queen could at last rejoin her anxious family.

Lafayette, thinking all was well, soon went off to bed, leaving the people camped in front of the palace, where, for lack of other food, some of them killed and ate one of the guard's horses. Then some of the rioters, unable to sleep on the hard stones, prowled around until they found a door open and unguarded, through which they entered the palace. Heated by drink for although they lacked bread, they never seemed to lack wine to excite them to commit deeds of violence, these men suddenly determined to kill Marie Antoinette, "the Austrian," "Madam Deficit," the cause of all their woes. They therefore boldly forced their way to her bedroom, two of her guards losing their lives in vain efforts to prevent their advance.

Fortunately, this struggle afforded the queen time to escape by a private passage to the king's room, just as the rioters burst into her chamber and began madly to thrust their swords and pikes through her curtains, blankets, and mattress. In fact, it was only when these were fairly riddled with holes, that the discovery was made that their hated victim was not there! The king, who was too soft-hearted to hurt anybody, and evidently unaware that "humanity to mobs often proves inhumanity to mankind," would not allow these men to be seized and punished, but had them coaxed out of the palace, to await morning and the promised departure of the royal family for Paris. Then, as he managed to delay the start until early afternoon, some of the mob set out in advance to announce his coming, bearing aloft as trophies the heads of the two murdered guards!

The journey to Paris was made terrible by the heat and dust, and by the coarse men and women who went with them all the way, shouting madly, "We are bringing the baker, the baker's wife, and the baker's boy!" and pointing in confirmation to fifty cartloads of grain which they had found in a royal granary. This journey was termed the "Joyous Entry" by the populace, but was nothing short of torture for the haughty queen, and was never forgotten by the royal children, who were frightened almost out of their senses. Versailles was now deserted—a fact made clear by a sign which expressed popular sentiments and read:—

> "Palace to rent,
>   Parliament for sale,
>   Ministers to hang,
>   Crown to give away!"

> *Palais a loner,*
>   *Parlement a vendre,*
>   *Ministres a pendre,*
>   *Couronne a donner!*

The royal family were never to live in Versailles again, but were instead to occupy the palace called the Tuileries in Paris, which had not been prepared for their coming, and where they were very uncomfortable at first. But after a while things got better, and their Majesties held there many conferences with prominent men, Mirabeau, especially, promising at last to do all he could to serve them.

Death of Mirabeau

The king having left Versailles, the National Assembly immediately transferred its headquarters to Paris, where it continued the work of making new laws for France. As money was badly needed, it was decreed that all church property should belong to the state, that part of it should be sold, and that many monasteries and convents should be closed. The monks and nuns thus made homeless, although told they were no longer bound by their vows, refused in many cases to be released from them, living on charity, or earning their bread as best they could in a wicked world.

On the other hand, it was decreed that all priests were henceforth to be paid by the state; but a later law rearranged the bishoprics, provided that bishops and priests should be chosen by the voters, and required all priests to take a "civic oath," or promise of fidelity to this law. As some of the clauses of this law conflicted with their previous vows, only about a tenth of the clergy would consent. The remainder were not allowed to continue in office, or even to give their services to stanch Catholics, who considered that priests who had taken the civic oath had committed perjury. This belief—shared by the king and queen—was upheld by a decree from the Pope, forbidding all priests to obey this order. The French government took its revenge by seizing and annexing Avignon (1790), which had belonged to the Holy See some four hundred and eighty-two years, and which now went to form one of the new departments into which the Assembly divided France, after abolishing the former provinces.

By confiscating the property of the church, which had naturally been growing wealthier as time went on, the state was vastly enriched. Still, as this property was mainly land, and could not be sold immediately, a sufficient amount of paper money was issued, the stipulation being made that purchasers should pay for church lands in paper money, which the authorities would destroy as soon as paid in.

The National Assembly also decreed the abolition of the irksome salt tax, the suppression of royal warrants, and the institution of regular juries.

In spite of all these innovations, popular agitation was not subsiding, for many political clubs had been founded,—clubs which took their names as a rule from the halls where they met (Jacobins, Cordeliers, Feuillants, etc.). In each of these assemblies, ardent and eloquent speakers aired their

Hall of the Jacobin Club

views, for now that the press and public speech were no longer hampered, all that had hitherto been suppressed, or only spoken of in whispers, was proclaimed openly.

When one year had elapsed after the fall of the Bastille (whose key, by the way, had been sent by Lafayette to Washington and is still at Mount Vernon), the people wished to celebrate this anniversary in a fitting manner. The "Federation Festival" was therefore planned and held on the Field of Mars, in front of the *Invalides* or Home for Veteran Soldiers. In the center of this immense parade ground was erected a mound of earth, on top of which was placed the "altar of the country." Around it were arranged tiers of grass seats, or terraces, from which spectators could view all that was going on. Talleyrand—a very clever but very unprincipled ex-priest—officiated at this altar, where Lafayette took the civic oath for the army, Bailly for the National Assembly, and the king publicly swore fidelity to the whole nation. The queen, who was present, then held up the little Dauphin, who swore, too, to the frantic delight of the people; and they, after having unanimously registered their own oaths, hurried off to dance on the site of the fallen Bastille! Thus, you see, all seemed satisfactory, for the king had apparently recovered the confidence and affection of his people, who even cheered his family; but this joyful demonstration was to be the last in favor of their Majesties, whose worst days were rapidly drawing near.

The coming of these evil times was hastened by the political clubs, which, while they undoubtedly did some good, also worked untold harm, for people who know naught of self-government cannot undertake it safely all at once. The fact was that, having been told that all men are equal, all wished to command, none were willing to serve or obey; even in the army, discipline became so lax that the troops at Nancy shot their own commander!

Necker, who had thrice been minister of finance in these troublous times, now withdrew in despair to his home in Switzerland, and his successor rashly proceeded to issue more paper money, this time without any proper guarantee. The money, however, was sorely needed to support the increased national forces, as well as to indemnify slave-owners in Haiti, where colored people were first enfranchised and granted political rights by the French government.

Early in the year 1791, the people made a grand demonstration in honor of the man whom they affectionately called "little Mother Mirabeau." Although still quite young, this man had led such a fast life that he had little strength left, and easily succumbed to disease. Because he made fine speeches almost to the very end, and because he said many noble things, such as "Right is sovereign of the world!" the people mourned his untimely death. They gave him a grand public funeral, burying him in the Church of the Pantheon, which, having been set aside as a resting place for national heroes, was then adorned with the inscription it still bears, "To great men, in the name of a grateful country." *(Aux grands hommes, la patrie reconnaissante.)* A little later the words "Liberty, Equality, Fraternity "*(Liberté, Egalité, Fraternité)* the usual formula of the French Republic—were added to the above dedication.

Mirabeau's death proved a great loss to the royal family, which ever since their arrival in Paris had been aware of the fact that they were being closely watched, and that spies lurked even among their body servants. They therefore had to exercise the utmost caution, often not daring to trust their letters to the public mails for fear they would be opened. For that reason, Marie Antoinette sent some of her ladies abroad with important papers, and especially with the keys for the ciphers she meant to use thereafter. These keys were for the king's brother and for her own brother, the Emperor of Austria, as well as for various trustworthy subjects and friends, who were to correspond with her in cipher.

In this manner, the king and queen secretly learned that the émigrés were furious at the tidings they received from France (the destruction of property, abolition of privileges, etc.), and that rulers of neighboring countries were becoming seriously uneasy lest the new French ideas should invade their realms also, and deprive them of power, like Louis XVI.

The Flight to Varennes

The king's brothers and the principal Royalists strongly advised the king to leave Paris, the center of the storm, and join the émigrés and the armies they were raising, so as to return to his capital with their aid and dictate terms instead of having them forced upon him. The royal family accordingly decided to depart; but, knowing that any open attempt to leave the city would be hindered, and would tend to make their situation even more unbearable, Louis XVI. decided to escape in disguise (June, 1791).

Unfortunately, far too elaborate preparations were made for this venture, so that the start was not made until six weeks after the decision was reached. Then the royal family stole out of the palace in small detachments, to join the great traveling coach which had been built for a Russian lady (Marie Antoinette), traveling with her two daughters (Madam Royal and the little Dauphin, disguised as a girl), a lackey (the king), and a maid (Madam Elizabeth, the king's sister). As all the roads were bad, and all vehicles very clumsy in those days, the great traveling carriage lumbered slowly on; still, all went well until the king, who naturally felt anxious, stuck his head out of the window, and was recognized by the well-known features stamped on every coin in his realm.

The man who thus discovered the royal flight just as the horses were being changed at a relay station, had no chance to stop the fugitives there. So he sprang on a horse, and, by a short cut, reached Varennes and roused its citizens before the arrival of the coach. It was at Varennes, also, that the king expected to meet a military escort, which would have protected him the rest of the way; but this escort, by some misunderstanding, was waiting patiently at one end of the town, while the king was arrested in the other by citizens hastily armed with any weapon they could procure. In spite of all Louis's entreaties to be allowed to continue, these sullen people would not let him go, declaring they had sent a messenger to Paris, and that he must await the orders of the Assembly.

The result was that two members were dispatched from Paris to bring back their Majesties, and home they went, escorted by a rabble nearly as repellent as the one which had brought them from Versailles the year before. The slow return journey was accomplished under the most uncomfortable circumstances, for in the carriage—full at starting—now sat also the two members of the Assembly, who constantly talked politics to their weary captives.

The queen had to hold the Dauphin in her lap all the way, and there was only one seat for the king's sister and daughter, who therefore took turns sitting in each other's lap. Throughout those long hours of anxiety and martyrdom, Marie Antoinette never uttered one word of complaint, but kept the six-year-old prince quiet by gently whispered words, which he always heeded, for he was a good child and simply adored his beautiful mother.

The dusty procession reached Paris at last, where they were received with dead silence, for the Assembly had decreed, "Whoever applauds the king shall be flogged; whoever insults him shall be hanged." On reentering their palace, where they were now openly guarded like dangerous prisoners, the royal family could at last rest, and were soon relieved to learn by secret means that the king's brother (who had started at the same time as they) had managed to escape, and that the queen's hairdresser had safely crossed the frontier with her jewels.

While the royal family was thus held in durance vile, the people buried Rousseau and Voltaire in the Pantheon with great pomp, and the Assembly finished drawing up the new constitution, which gave the lawmaking power to an elective Legislative Assembly, and left the king only the power to veto (forbid) the execution of any new law for four years. Nevertheless, the long-suffering monarch accepted this code (Sept. 14, 1790), publicly swearing to obey it. Of course, the king and deputies knew what all the words in this constitution meant, but the common people, who had no education, were greatly mystified, especially by the word "veto." Still, there always are persons ready to explain even what they do not understand, and the following dialogue, overheard between two peasants, indicates the general belief among the mob:—

"Do you know what the veto is?"

"No."

"Ah, well! you have your porringer full of soup. The king says to you, 'Pour out that soup,' and you have to pour it out!"

"Ah! down with the veto then! down with the veto!"

As "veto" was thus taken to mean something hateful and objectionable, the people began to call Marie Antoinette "Madam Veto," in addition to the other horrid names they had already bestowed upon her.

You cannot wonder, therefore, that trembling constantly for the lives of her husband and children, the queen kept urging her brother to help them, and implored the French nobles to do their duty and come and defend their king. One of her messages was, "If you love your king, your religion, your government, and your country, return! return! return!"

When the framing of the constitution was finished, the National Assembly dissolved, to make room for the new Legislative Assembly, to which, by a strange provision, none of the members of the former body were eligible. Thus some very good men were excluded from government affairs, while some of the most rabid club men came to the front in their stead. This Legislative Assembly remained in power nearly twelve months. The various parties in it were called, from the seats they occupied, "the Right," "the Left," "the Mountain" (highest seats), and "the Center." As some of its members were in favor of a constitutional monarchy, others of a republic, and as some were even what we should now call Communists, you can readily imagine that lively times were in store.

The news of the captivity of the royal family, and especially of a constitution depriving the king of practically all rights,—as well as of the titles "Sire" and "Your Majesty,"—caused a great sensation abroad, and induced Prussia and Austria to sign a treaty, whereby they bound themselves to help Louis XVI. recover his power. But before these intentions could be carried out, the Austrian Emperor died, and was succeeded by his son, a nephew of Marie Antoinette. Meantime, the fact that any European nation dared purpose to step in and tell the French government what should be done, so enraged a hot-headed people that war was immediately declared, and troops hastily dispatched to the northeastern frontier, the most liable to attack. Some regiments were therefore stationed at Strassburg, where the mayor—giving a dinner to a few officers—happened to remark, that it was a great pity there were now no patriotic songs for the soldiers to sing, the old ones not being suited to the new constitution.

This remark was overheard by Rouget de l'Isle, one of the guests, who, unable to sleep that night, and haunted by the desire to supply the necessary song, sat up all night, composing the words and tune of what was to be a famous national song. He was not aware of the fact that it was wonderful in any way until he sang it the next day to the mayor,—one of whose daughters played the accompaniment for him,—and saw tears of emotion flow from the eyes of all present. The mayor immediately had some copies of this song printed and sent in various directions. One sheet reached Marseilles just as a regiment was leaving for Paris. It was sung to the men, who enthusiastically roared it on their march to Paris, thus popularizing the new tune, which every one then thought had originated in the great southern French port. Hence it was called "la Marseillaise".

Rouget de Lisle sings "la Marseillaise". - Isidore Pils

Meantime, the king had further estranged the people by unwisely vetoing several laws passed by the Assembly. Besides, the mob—who were not fit to join the army, but were still out of work, and lacking everything except strong drink—were listening to every rumor, and distorting every fact they did not understand. They were ready to rush madly here or there at short notice, at the command of their leaders, many of whom were saloon-keepers, brigands, and criminals of the lowest class, men, in short, whom it would have been far wiser to clap in prison. These people wore rudely shaped trousers with blouses or carters' frocks coming down to their knees,—the latter garment being even the only one worn by some of the poorest,—besides the red liberty cap (the old Roman sign of an enfranchised slave), and clogs or wooden shoes. It was only the well-to-do in France who could afford the knee breeches so fashionable in those days, because such garments made necessary long stockings, which were very costly before machinery was invented to manufacture them in quantities. But as the aristocrats who had fled at the first sign of trouble were deeply scorned by the mob, the rabble now proudly termed themselves the "men without breeches," or *sans-culottes*, a name which they delighted to flaunt in the face of the foe.

Mobs Raid the Tuileries

The old adage, "Satan finds some mischief still for idle hands to do," is well exemplified by the actions of the Paris mob at this time. When the news suddenly came that Prussian and Austrian forces had beaten the French army, all France was instantly in a turmoil. The clubs in Paris cried that treason was at work, and the mob, always ascribing everything evil to king and queen, immediately rushed off to the Tuileries to call them to account. Instead of banners,—the red flag of liberty now generally replaced the white of royalty,—they brandished aloft on this occasion a pair of trousers, with the inscription *"Sans Culottes,"* an ox heart marked "Heart of an Aristocrat," and a miniature gallows, from which dangled a doll boldly labeled "Marie Antoinette". Roaring out at the top of their lungs the popular "ca ira", and dancing the "Carmagnole",—a wild jig interspersed with all manner of rough cries and oaths,—they rushed on to the palace, where they soon broke in and scattered in search of their Majesties. Discovering the king alone in one room, the mob immediately began to demand this and that, to which Louis XVI. calmly replied, "I will do all the constitution prescribes," but would promise nothing further. Thinking he might feel frightened,—and any one might under such circumstances,—one man, who had given the king a red cap to put on, said reassuringly, Fear nothing, Sire, I will protect you!" But he was greatly surprised when he received the prompt reply: "Do you think I fear? Place your hand upon my heart. You will find no quick beatings of terror there." Still, the king good-naturedly accepted the glass of wine which another man offered him, and stood patiently for hours while the mob filed past him.

He was not the only brave person in the palace, however. The mob, having found his sister, began to insult her, thinking she was the queen, and when some one near her attempted to explain the mistake, Madam Elizabeth imploringly whispered, "Do not undeceive them!" for she hoped to spare one pang at least to the poor sister-in-law whom she loved so dearly. The mob, pressing ever onward, finally discovered their error, and crowded angrily around the queen and her two children. To protect them and herself from the repulsive throng, Marie Antoinette placed her son on a table, behind which she and her daughter could stand, and with hands that did not tremble, fitted a red liberty cap on the Dauphin's golden curls. It was then and there that the following pathetic dialogue took place:—

Marie Antoinette. "Have I ever done you any harm?"

Woman. "No, but you are the cause of the misery of the nation!"

Marie Antoinette. "You have been told so, but you are mistaken. As the wife of the King of France, and the mother of the Dauphin, I am a Frenchwoman. I shall never see my country again. I can be happy only in France. I was happy when you loved me."

Woman. "I beg your pardon. It was because I did not know you. I see that you are good."

This raid on the Tuileries was witnessed by a young officer, Napoleon Bonaparte, who, gazing at the wild mob from a street corner near by, is said to have muttered: "Why have they admitted all that rabble? They ought to sweep off four or five hundred of them with cannon; the rest would run fast enough!" As you will see, this officer never hesitated to mow down people with grapeshot, for he was never troubled with too great sympathy for others, and could easily kill a few hundred without remorse,—a thing kindly Louis could never countenance.

The news of the invasion of the palace, and of the royal family's danger, roused the utmost indignation abroad, where talk of a coalition of all the European nations was now frequently heard. The French, realizing therefore that they were likely to be attacked on all sides at once, immediately declared the country in danger, and called for volunteers, who, fired by patriotism, enlisted in hosts.

It was shortly after the second celebration of the Federation Festival (three years after the fall of the Bastille) that the Marseilles troops marched into Paris, singing "the Marseillaise," just in time to take part in a second invasion of the Tuileries (Aug. 10, 1792), instead of maintaining order in the capital, as had been expected. This time, as there had been some warning of the mob's coming, cannon were set in place and loaded, while eight hundred Swiss guards and twelve hundred nobles stood ready to defend the royal family at the king's order. But Louis XVI., knowing how ignorant and misled the majority of the rioters were, had not the heart to use decisive means and to shed blood. He therefore again forbade using the cannon, and allowed the mob to invade the palace.

45

As the rabble, this time, seemed even more excited than the last, the king announced that he and his family would leave the palace by the rear, cross the garden, and place themselves under the protection of the Legislative Assembly, to prevent bloodshed. Some say that Louis XVI. sent word to his Swiss guards that he was leaving, bidding them offer no resistance; others declare that the order was forgotten or transmitted only to part of the force. However that may be, the inrushing mob slew most of the king's defenders, who died fighting bravely. Their heroic death is commemorated by the "Lion of Lucerne," in Switzerland, carved in the living rock by the Danish sculptor Thorvaldsen.

Meantime, the royal family had crossed the garden,—the little Dauphin playfully kicking the dead leaves before him,—and had entered the Legislative Assembly, where they were kept waiting some time in the corridor, although the king announced immediately on arriving, "I have come here to prevent a great crime." Then they were finally allowed to sit in the reporter's box, where they suffered from heat, confinement, hunger, and thirst, until the Assembly announced that the king should be "suspended," and that, for safe keeping, he and his family should be committed to the great fortress called the Temple.

The Lion of Lucerne (Image by CoolCaesar)

There, instead of occupying the luxurious apartments recently inhabited by princes, they were put in the prison tower, where every comfort was lacking, and whence only one of them was to come out again free. Five days later Lafayette, who had hitherto done his best to maintain order and discipline; secretly left France, and it was well he did so, for hundreds of the king's friends were now being thrown into prison. House-to-house visits were being made to discover and imprison all "suspects"; that is to say, all aristocrats, and the priests who maintained their allegiance to the Pope and Church, and who might hence be inclined to give aid or information to the foe.

Members of the Aristocracy Taken for Execution

These people, and the few faithful subjects who had followed the king and queen to the Temple only to be parted from them, were locked up in various prisons, where, on the first few days of September, a terrible massacre took place, hundreds of priests and aristocrats being cruelly butchered by volunteer assassins hired by the city government of Paris—part of the mob which had twice invaded the Tuileries. These "September Massacres" were suggested by Danton, whose motto was, "Dare, dare again, dare ever," and were brutally urged by Marat, for the people had declared, "We must leave no traitors behind us when we hasten to the frontier," and every priest and aristocrat loyal to the king was now viewed as a traitor to his country.

Only the most rudimentary trial was given to these unfortunates, nearly all of whom were led out and promptly put to death by four hundred tiger-like cutthroats! Madame de Lamballe, the queen's virtuous and beautiful friend, was hacked to pieces, and her head was borne off on a pike to be exhibited in triumph to the prisoners in the Temple. But a merciful fainting fit saved Marie Antoinette from this ghastly sight, which horrified the king when he gazed curiously out of a window to discover the cause of the sudden tumult.

Many thrilling stories are told of the courage and devotion shown during these awful days. One daughter, it is said, saved her father by pleading with the judges, offering her own life in exchange for his; and another young lady, having no alternative, saved her father by drinking a glass of the blood of one of the freshly slain victims!

The Battle of Valmy

But popular rage was turned to delirious joy when, a few days later, the French general Dumouriez won the battle of Valmy, just as the Legislative Assembly was ending its work and the National Convention entered upon its duties. The latter body had been elected to frame a new constitution for France, and it remained in control of the government for three years. This Convention—which had the honor of founding a School for Arts and Crafts, a Normal School, and a Polytechnic School, of introducing the metric system and the signal telegraph (semaphore), besides giving France a new calendar—began its sittings by formally deposing Louis XVI. and proclaiming the First French Republic (Sept. 21, 1792) "one and indivisible." A decree of perpetual banishment was passed against the émigrés, who were forbidden to return to France on pain of death.

A few days later French armies conquered Savoy and Nice, and the allies, beaten on all sides, were forced to withdraw from France. Then patriotic hearts soon after were gladdened by the news of another victory at Jemappes (1792), a triumph which secured Belgium, and went to the heads of the Revolutionists to such an extent that the Convention now boldly declared, "The French will treat as enemies any nation which, refusing liberty and equality, desires to preserve its princes and privileged castes, or to make any compromise with them!"

The King's Trial

It did not seem enough, however, to dethrone poor King Louis XVI., for he was now to be called to account for the sins of his fathers. His ordeal began by his being separated from his family, with whom he had been living within the Temple walls during the past five months. Next, he was summoned before the Convention to be tried, where all former respectful modes of address were discarded, and he was bluntly addressed as "Louis," or "Louis Capet." While he was allowed a lawyer,—who pleaded eloquently in his behalf and did his utmost to save him,—the Convention had so thoroughly made up its mind in advance to condemn him, that even slow-witted Louis perceived it, for he said, "They will bring me to the scaffold, but no matter, I shall gain my cause if I leave an unspotted memory behind me!" And his lawyer once despairingly exclaimed, "I seek judges in you, and find nothing but accusers!"

Everything that could be trumped up against his poor Majesty was now brought to light, and his weakness in often changing his mind was made a capital crime. Papers were produced which were said to have been found in an iron box hidden in his palace wall, and which proved that the king had been corresponding with his brothers and other émigrés, as well as with Austria, begging them to lend him their assistance in his sore straits.

While it was a foregone conclusion that he would be found guilty, it may be that Louis's life might yet have been spared, had not Danton suggested, referring to the foes of France, "Let us throw them the head of a king as gage of battle!" As soon as the trial was over, votes were taken on several questions, each member stepping forward to proclaim aloud his opinion. First, the king was found guilty by an almost unanimous vote; but then, on the question of his punishment, there was only a small majority in favor of death. The voting and speech making lasted several days; for many members insisted on giving their reasons for their votes. Every one present shuddered when the king's cousin—the former Duke of Orleans, who now prided himself upon bearing the name of Philip Equality (Philippe Egalite)—stepped boldly forward and said, "With a single regard to my duty, I vote for death." Another member, Sieyes, who harshly voted, "Death, without explanations!" had an unpleasant reminder of this brutal remark when, later on, as ambassador at Berlin, he invited a member of the royal family to dinner, only to receive the curt reply, "No, without explanations!"

The last question to be voted on was whether the execution should be delayed. It was then that Thomas Paine, an American residing in Paris, who was a member of the Convention, made a formal protest in the name of his country, saying, "The man whom you condemn to death is regarded by the people of the United States as their best friend, as the founder of liberty!" But a majority of seventy decided against delay, and the Convention ordered that Louis be guillotined within twenty-four hours. (The guillotine was a machine recently invented by a Frenchman for the work of beheading.)

While the voting was going on, Louis was in another room, calmly meditating. When the news was brought to him, he gravely said, "For two hours past I have been considering whether, during my whole reign, I have voluntarily given any cause of complaint to my subjects, and with perfect sincerity I now declare that I deserve no reproach at their hands, and that I have never formed a wish but for their happiness."

This statement made no difference; the cruel sentence was read, to which Louis offered no protest. He made no moan, but asked permission to take leave of his family, and to have the aid of a priest of his own choice to prepare for death. Both these favors were granted; but as Louis would not have a French priest who had renounced allegiance to the Pope, and could not have any other French clergyman, he had to accept the aid of Abbe Edgeworth, an English priest then residing in France.

The King's Execution

As the end was so near, Louis XVI.'s last painful interview with his family took place that selfsame evening, under the supervision of the brutal jailers who guarded them. For two hours the royal family wept together, embracing one another, and speaking their last farewells. Louis took his little son on his knee, and so impressively told him he must forgive his oppressors, that, young as he was,—not quite eight years old,—the little fellow remembered and obeyed even under the most trying circumstances.

When the two hours were over and he saw they must part, Louis pacified his wife and sister by promising to see them again on the morrow, although he knew this was the last glimpse he would have, in this world, of the defenseless beings he loved so dearly, and to whom he had always been a good husband, father, and brother. Marie Antoinette, who now never resented anything that was done to her, indignantly exclaimed to her husband's jailers as she passed them going out from this heartrending interview, "You are all rascals!"—a reproof which cut deep because it was so true, and for which they never forgave her.

Place de la Concorde.

The affecting parting with his family once over, Louis XVI.,—who had already written his will,—had nothing to do but prepare for the end. He therefore spent most of the night in prayer, sleeping only a little while, and that mainly because he did not wish to appear tired, or to have his courage give out at the end through bodily weakness.

The next morning, after confessing and receiving the last sacrament, Louis begged pardon of his jailer, with whom he had been impatient the day before,—intrusted his last messages for his family to the faithful servant who had followed him to prison, handed his will to the commissioners, and himself gave the signal for departure. A moment later, his poor wife heard the carriage drive away, and then only learned that she was not to see him again before he died! All the streets were lined with troops, and the city absolutely silent, so no sound save the roll of the wheels over the pavement distracted the king's thoughts from his final prayers. Realizing that his faith was now his sole stay and consolation, he exclaimed,

"Where should I be now if God had not granted me grace to remain true to my religion?"

On reaching the scaffold,—erected opposite the Tuileries, on the spot where one of the fountains of the Place de la Concorde now plays,—Louis XVI. stepped out of his carriage, and after recommending his confessor to the care of the executioners, promptly divested himself of his coat. But when they attempted to bind his hands, he resisted indignantly, saying: "Tie my hands! No, I will not submit to this. Do your duty, but do not attempt to tie me. You shall not do it!" But the men insisted, and the king's confessor now whispered, "Sire, this last insult will only provide a fresh point of resemblance between your Majesty and the God who will be your recompense!" Louis then ceased to resist, and rejoined with a sigh: Assuredly, His example alone could induce me to submit to such an indignity. Do as you please; I will drink the cup to the dregs."

It was, therefore, with hands fast bound behind him, that Louis XVI stepped forward to the railing, and, facing the assembled crowd, cried in a firm voice: "I die innocent of the crimes imputed to me. I forgive the authors of my death, and I pray that my blood may not fall upon France. . . ." But here his speech was interrupted by loud rolls of the drums, the authorities fearing lest a reaction should take place in his favor even at the last minute.

A moment later, just after Abbe Edgeworth is reported to have pronounced the famous words, "Son of St. Louis, ascend to Heaven!" the executioner exhibited the king's head to the multitude, who gazed in awestruck silence at the countenance of the last of the unbroken line of thirty-three Capetian kings who had, so far, ruled France.

Then people crowded around the scaffold, to dip their handkerchiefs in the king's blood, some of these relics being still piously preserved. But, instead of resting from the first in St. Denis,—where a monument was erected later over what could still be found of his remains,—Louis XVI. was buried like other guillotine victims, in the spot where now rises a beautiful chapel, the *Chapelle Expiatoire*, erected in atonement of this sinful execution of an innocent king, and of many other victims. Louis, the best but weakest of the Bourbons, died thus at thirty-eight, after a reign of eighteen and a half years; but although his foes had clamored for his death, saying, "Only the dead never come back to trouble us," he was to prove far more formidable to them dead than alive, for since the French had made a martyr of him, all Europe rose up to avenge his death.

Story of Charlotte Corday

"The Tyrant," as the Revolutionists styled poor Louis XVI., was no more, and the news of his death reached the ears of his stricken family only by means of news-vender's cries. Thus also it became known to his eldest brother,—one of the émigrés,—who immediately proclaimed the captive Dauphin, Louis XVII., assuming himself the title of Regent—because Monarchists, of course, did not accept the decree of the Convention that there should be no more royalty in France.

The new Republic, meantime, had its hands very full, for all Europe was rising up against it, the Revolution being everywhere considered as a menace to law and order. The French Royalists, too, were ready to rebel, those in the northwest being particularly rabid, as they were anxious to avenge both their king and the Church. They therefore organized what is known in history as the Insurrection of the Vendee, an uprising in and near Brittany, headed by very brave leaders. Composed of a few nobles, and of many peasants,—who were armed at first merely with scythes and pitchforks, and hooted like screech owls to signal to each other,—this royalist force carried on a guerrilla warfare in that wild section of the country for about three years. These Vendee royalists or Chouans (meaning "screech owls"), many thousands of whom gave their lives for their cause, were also known as the Whites, because they rallied around the royal standard, while their opponents, the Republicans, were known as the Blues, and proudly bore the flag which France now uses.

With so many enemies without and within, immediate measures of defense were imperative, so, while Carnot began to raise armies, Danton organized a Revolutionary Tribunal, before which "suspects" were brought and summarily judged. There was no appeal from its decrees, and as it had scores of branches in different parts of the country, no enemy of the Republic could hope to escape. Finally, the Convention intrusted all public authority to a secret Committee of Public Safety, consisting of nine able and active members. One of them, Danton, had said, "Let the reign of terror be the order of the day!" and this bloodthirsty remark furnishes the name for the darkest epoch of French history, the Reign of Terror, extending from June 2, 1793, to July 17, 1794, fourteen dreadful months!

Among those who were not satisfied with the way things were being conducted, was General Dumouriez,—the victor of Valmy and Jemappes,—who wished to restore monarchy in France, although in favor of a son of the Duke of Orleans, and not of poor little Louis XVII. When the Convention began to suspect him, after his defeat at Neerwinden, four commissioners were sent to his camp to question and, if need be, arrest him. Dumouriez, on hearing what these men had to say, exclaimed, "The tigers want my head, but I won't give it to them!" Then he turned the tables by having the commissioners summarily handed over to the Austrians, to be detained in their camp as hostages, and, after vainly trying to induce his army to follow him, he and his royal protégé (later King Louis Philippe) went over to the enemy, too.

During April and May, 1793, one reads of nothing but accusations, arrests, and riots, for the whole country was in a terrible ferment, the passions in Paris, in particular, being constantly at the boiling point. Then, early in June, thirty-four members of the Convention—known as the Girondists, because they came mostly from the Gironde—were proscribed by order of the two leaders now most influential, Marat and Robespierre, their main crime being heroic attempts to restrain the bloodthirsty element in the country. Some of the Girondists managed to escape, and fled to Lyons, Caen, and elsewhere; but more than a score were arrested and imprisoned to await trial.

The Girondists who escaped began to raise armies, using all their eloquence against their foes. Their denunciations so fired Charlotte Corday,—a girl of twenty-five, living at Caen,—that, pretending a voyage to England, she took leave of her family and betook herself to Paris. There, she intended to rid her beloved country of the monster whom she deemed the author of all its woes. So, on the pretext that she had information of importance to convey, she obtained admission to Marat's presence, although he was then suffering from a skin disease which caused such intense irritation that he was in the habit of spending most of his time in a medicated bath. To enable him to write for his paper, *The People's Friend*, and also to receive his many visitors, Marat lay in a covered bathtub, from which only his head and right arm emerged.

When the beautiful young woman was ushered in, Marat invited her to sit down beside him, and began eagerly inquiring the names of the deputies who had taken refuge at Caen. He had just written down the last, and was saying in a tone of grim satisfaction that their heads would soon fall, when Charlotte Corday, drawing a dagger from the folds of her kerchief, drove it deep into his heart! A moment later the dauntless girl, seized by Marat's servants, was dragged off to prison, but at her trial she calmly testified: "I wished to put a stop to the civil war, and to offer up my life for the good of my country. I have no accomplices."

Tried and found guilty, Charlotte Corday was condemned to be guillotined, but faced death with great fortitude, convinced that her deed had been fully as praiseworthy as that of Jael or Judith. And, although at that time people so

54

admired Marat that they solemnly buried him in the Pantheon, like a great patriot, they changed their minds about him even before the Revolution was over, and removed his remains to another, less conspicuous resting place.

Meanwhile, the Girondists had stirred up rebellions in several parts of France, which were later put down with the utmost cruelty. At Lyons, as the guillotine could not work fast enough, the rebels were bunched together and mowed down in crowds with grapeshot. As for the city, it was almost destroyed, and this inscription was placed on a mound of ruins, "Lyons made war against Liberty,—Lyons is no more!" Such an example, as you may well imagine, struck terror into the hearts of all, and the cry now became, "Liberty, Equality, Fraternity, or Death!"

Toulon, which the rebels had turned over to the English, was closely besieged by Republican troops. It was at this siege that Bonaparte—then a young lieutenant of artillery—pointed out the spot from which batteries could best command the enemy's position, thereby securing for the Republic a decisive advantage in the struggle for this important city. Bonaparte's unusual abilities were then and there seen and recognized by Barras, a member of the Convention, who, as you will see, was later to give this young officer a chance to distinguish himself as general in the French army.

Meantime, the Convention had been at work upon a new constitution for France, "the Constitution of 1793," which, though finished and adopted in that year, was never put into effect; instead, the Convention and its Committee of Public Safety continued to rule.

The Queen Parted from her Children

You may have been wondering what had become of poor Marie Antoinette, whom we left in prison, just after learning that her husband was dead. This fatal news plunged the queen into such a state of stony grief, that only the sudden and severe illness of her little fourteen-year-old daughter saved her from becoming insane. This poor girl—"the little Madam" as some of the more compassionate guards sometimes ventured to call her, although the majority used only the rough "citizeness" of the times—did not die, however, but recovered to help her aunt amuse poor little Louis. They two played with him, gave him his lessons, waited upon Marie Antoinette, and kept their rooms tidy, for they now had no attendant to undertake that care.

Marie Antoinette never doubted at this time that help would soon be forthcoming, and that her son would yet reign over France, for, since his father was dead, she naturally considered him king. The Royalists were, meantime, most anxious to secure possession of their monarch, and, knowing the mob's ferocity and hatred, longed to rescue the queen also. They therefore devised many plots to rescue the royal captives, but were always baffled. Besides, the queen did not wish to escape without her children, or to let them go without her, for she now felt it unsafe to trust any one.

Mainly because Marie Antoinette viewed her son as the King of France, the Convention decreed that he should be taken from her, and intrusted to the care of a "tutor" of their own selection. One night, therefore, after Marie Antoinette had tenderly put her little son to bed, officers suddenly appeared, demanding his custody. The mother, frantic with grief, stood before the bed, defending him fiercely, and it was only when the officers seriously threatened to kill both her children, that she finally yielded in despair.

The good aunt and the poor little sister had to dress the weeping and frightened child. Then Marie Antoinette, herself, handed him over to the officers, after bidding the poor little fellow: "Always remember, my son, a mother who loves you. Be good, gentle, and true!" He was never to see his beloved mother again.

Louis was at once committed to the care of a rough shoemaker named Simon, who, though well paid, resented being locked up in the Temple to watch him, and who sometimes vented his spite upon this innocent lad by illtreating him. Sworn at, beaten, and kicked because he cried for his mother, often roused by some rough order when he fell asleep, badgered even when trying to say his prayers, and forced to learn oaths and ribald songs in selfdefense, the poor little boy suffered actual martyrdom. He was only eight years old, remember, and had hitherto been treated with the utmost love and consideration. His poor mother had foreseen that he might fall into very brutal hands, but fortunately she never knew just how much he had to suffer, nor could she even imagine that Simon and his friends would force a child to drink bad liquor—as they sometimes did, knowing it was only when drunk that he could be made to sing the coarse songs they delighted to hear.

Throughout all this torture the little prince proved patient, gentle, and obedient, pathetically trying by small attentions and services to placate Simon and his coarse wife. He so constantly remembered his father's last words that once when his jailer, after taunting him to the utmost, curiously asked what he would do if he were free and king, the boy promptly and firmly replied, "I would forgive you!" Taken up daily to the top of the tower for air, Louis always paused at his mother's door, pleading vainly with eloquent glances—for he no longer dared ask—to be allowed to see her. Two or three times, through cracks in the wall, the poor mother had a glimpse of this idolized son, before the officers again appeared in the middle of the night, this time to lead her away!

There was no resistance now. After dressing herself quietly in the presence of the men who refused to leave her room even for a minute, Marie Antoinette bade her daughter and sister-in-law farewell, imploring the latter to watch over the children in her stead. The queen was then led to another prison (the Conciergerie), where she was conducted along a narrow corridor, so low and dark that we are told she struck her head a terrible blow. One officer, a trifle more humane than the rest, inquiring whether she had hurt herself, then received the broken-hearted reply, "Oh, no, nothing can hurt me any more!" From the end of July until the middle of October, Marie Antoinette was kept here in a cell, so damp and unwholesome that her clothes rotted, and that her one pair of shoes was always covered with mildew. Besides, lest any attempt should be made to rescue her, she was constantly guarded. Toward the last three men stayed in her cell night and day, drinking, smoking, swearing, playing cards, and constantly prying upon her every motion. With no tidings of her children, no means of occupation, and only one small book of devotion, the poor queen, who was always polite and gentle, and who never uttered a word of complaint, suffered, and was still.

While she was there, one attempt was made to rescue her, but as it was discovered, it only served to redouble the watchfulness and cruelty of her guards, thus making her situation worse instead of better.

Death of Marie Antoinette

In the middle of October, the queen—again without warning—was summoned before the Tribunal to be tried, no time being given to her to prepare any defense, while her enemies had craftily made all their plans to condemn her. For instance, a commission had even been sent to the Temple, to question the prince and both princesses.

Poor little Louis, dazed already by Simon's rough treatment, said "yes" to anything these men chose to ask. Then his sister was summoned, and entered the room, terrified at being alone with men for the first time in her young life; but, perceiving suddenly her small brother, she darted forward rapturously to embrace him, only to be cruelly prevented from doing so by the officers, who now proceeded to question her, too. Six years older, and therefore wiser and braver than the boy, Madam Royal gave them no satisfaction, although they cross-questioned her a long, long time, and did all they could to frighten her. But, while they did succeed in wringing tears from this little heroine, they could not obtain one word which could ever be used against her beloved mother. Next the aunt was called, whom these coarse men could not brow-beat as they had the children, and from whom, also, they could not wring anything save expressions of love and deep admiration for her poor brother's widow.

At her trial, Marie Antoinette was accused of meddling with the government, of giving her husband bad advice, and of considering her son king, although the Republic had been proclaimed! She was also asked to reveal what she knew in regard to certain so-called plots against the nation, giving the names of those who had taken part in them; but Marie Antoinette was no craven telltale, and all her judges obtained was the noble answer: "I shall never inform against my subjects. I have seen all, understood all, and forgotten all!" Then the old story of the Diamond Necklace, and all the other slanders spread by her enemies, were again brought to light, and, as if she could not be spared a single pang, the poor queen was told that her little son had accused her of trying to corrupt his morals.

To all these charges Marie Antoinette answered briefly or not at all, and, when urged to reply to the last, indignantly exclaimed, "I appeal to every mother here present, whether such a thing is possible!" This bold retort won such applause, even from hostile hearers, that the judges, fearing lest she should win the sympathy of the mob at the last minute, went on hurriedly with the business on hand. While thus questioned and badgered, hour after hour, she remained cool and dignified, saying pathetically toward the last: I was a queen and you took away my crown; a wife, and you killed my husband; a mother, and you robbed me of my children. My blood alone remains; take it, but do not make me suffer too long!" You see, she knew it was her life that these wretches were determined to have, so she was not surprised when the verdict "guilty" was given, and she was condemned to die within twenty-four hours.

Taken back to her unwholesome prison, Marie Antoinette spent the night writing a touching letter to Madam Elizabeth, imploring her to watch over the orphaned children. This letter, in which the queen forgave all her enemies, and begged her children never to try to avenge her, was not delivered to Madam Elizabeth, but was found among the cruel judge's papers when he was guillotined in his turn. It is now one of the precious historic relics of the country, and a copy of it is engraved in marble in the *Chapelle Expiatoire*. After her sentence had again been read to her in prison, Marie Antoinette made her last toilet,—still watched by her jailers— gen-

Marie Antoinette Led to Execution

tly thanking the young actress who gave her a clean white dress to wear. Next the chief executioner entered, cut off her beautiful hair, which he

58

burned, and bound her hands behind her so tightly that the cords actually cut into her tender flesh!

Louis XVI. had been taken to the scaffold in a carriage, and had been allowed the services of an orthodox priest; Marie Antoinette had to ride in a tumbrel, or cart, where she sat on a rude board beside a Constitutional priest (one who had taken the civic oath), the only kind of clergy now allowed to attend prisoners. Knowing the feelings of the people, Marie Antoinette feared they might attack and tear her to pieces before she could reach the scaffold. The priest, seeing this, tried to reassure her, and then, wishing to improve the occasion, began, "Madame, by your death you will expiate . . ."

"Yes," she interrupted quickly, *"errors*, but not *crimes!"* She was right: she had made mistakes, but only those natural to youth and ignorance, and had never committed any of the willful crimes which her foes laid to her charge.

Amid silence at first, and then a roar of insults, Marie Antoinette passed for the last time through the streets of Paris, and on reaching the scaffold sprang up the steps so eagerly that she dropped one of her slippers, which is now preserved as a sacred relic. On her way to the plank to which she was to be bound, she accidentally stepped on the executioner's foot, and apologized immediately, for her sufferings had made her even more tender of the feelings of others. As soon as the cruel knife had fallen, the executioner held the head of this victim so that all could gaze upon her features,—as he had done with that of her husband nine months before,—and then the remains of this Queen of France were buried by the state at a cost of less than two dollars.

The very day and hour that Marie Antoinette was thus released from a life which had been full of bliss and of sorrow, of grandeur and of bitter humiliation, the French won the battle of Wattignies (1793), and the nation thus claimed it had two causes for great rejoicing! The execution of Marie Antoinette was closely followed by that of twenty-one patriotic Girondists, who, on their way to the scaffold, and while awaiting their turn, heroically sang the "Marseillaise," to prove their devotion to their native country. Only one of their number dared not face the ordeal of the guillotine; but although he succeeded in committing suicide, his inanimate corpse was nevertheless borne to the scaffold to be beheaded with the rest. The strong chorus of a score of manly voices dwindled gradually as one head after another fell beneath the knife, but even the last Girondist kept up the strain, undaunted to the final minute.

The Duke of Orleans—who, you remember, had voted for his cousin's death, and who had since been equally execrated by both parties—was one of the next victims. He was sent to the scaffold with a criminal, who cried, "I hardly regret life, since he who has ruined my country receives the just punishment of his crimes, but what mortifies me is to be obliged to die on the same scaffold with him!"

Four days after this execution, Madame Roland,—the clever wife of the president of the Convention,—who for two years past had entertained the Girondists at her house, was also led to the scaffold. She had been an enthusiastic advocate of the Revolution at first, expecting that reforms would be effected in an orderly manner, as did the ardent patriots who formed her circle of literary and political friends.

During her imprisonment, Madame Roland spent her time writing her *Memoirs*, which are considered a graphic account of those times. Upon being condemned to die, she said to the judge who pronounced her sentence: "I thank you for having found me worthy to share the lot of the great men you have murdered. I shall try to display the same courage on the scaffold." To one of her former guests, brought to the scaffold with her, she quickly whispered, "Mount first; you would not have nerve enough to see me die." And when about to lay her own head under the knife, she is reported to have exclaimed, gazing at a statue of Liberty recently erected near there, "O Liberty, what crimes are committed in thy name!" Her husband, who managed to escape his pursuers and hide, was so maddened by grief at the news of her execution, that he committed suicide, protesting that he "would no longer remain in a world defiled by such crimes."

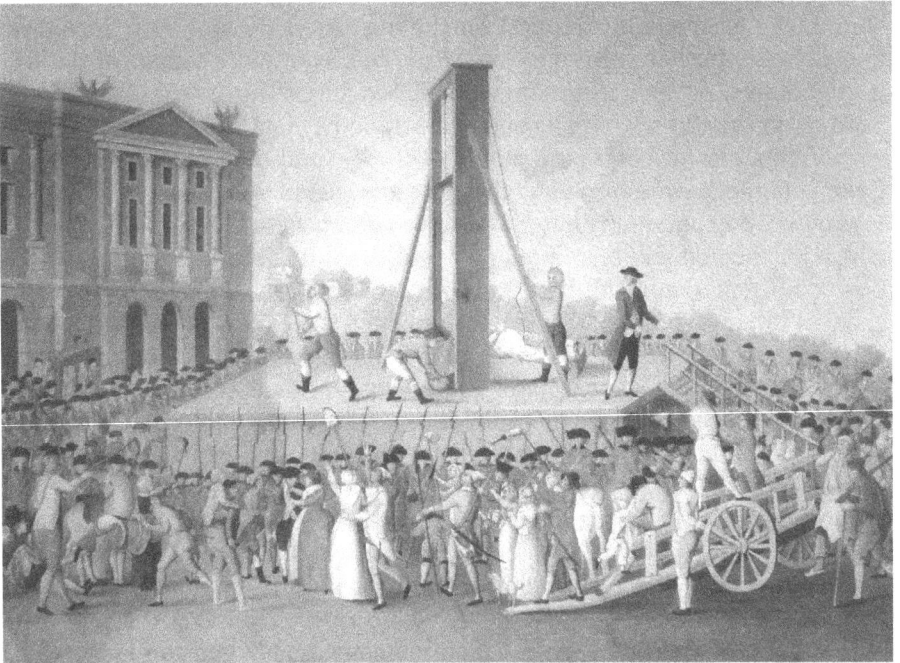

Many Executions

The end of the year 1793 was marked by a new change; namely, the formal abolishment of Christian religion in some parts of France, and the introduction of the "Worship of Reason." Many of the Revolutionists pretended not to believe in God, or in any life to come, so these men—Hebert and his followers—wrote over the gates of cemeteries, "Death is an eternal sleep," and decreed that the Church of Notre Dame should henceforth be used as the Temple of Reason. Their new worship was introduced by a pageant, an actress of the lowest type being dressed up like Minerva, placed on a golden chariot, and dragged into the building sanctified by many centuries of real devotion. There, all bowed down before the new goddess, while young girls strewed flowers before her, singing hymns. The whole ceremony was a ghastly parody of the religious ceremonies in the past, and shocked all good Christians, Catholic or Protestant, although no one dared express all one felt in such dangerous times.

Meantime, the siege of Toulon had been going on; and before the year closed, the Republic, thanks to Bonaparte, recovered possession of that port. One day during that siege Bonaparte called for a man to write under his dictation. Junot, a young officer, volunteered his services, and just as he finished writing, a cannon ball, striking near by, scattered dirt over his paper. Without changing color, Junot laughingly exclaimed, "Good! I shall not need any sand!" (In those days, sand was shaken over one's paper, to absorb extra ink, for blotters were not yet invented.) His coolness on this occasion not only attracted Bonaparte's attention, but won his genuine admiration. And Junot fully returned that feeling, for he said a little later, "General Bonaparte is one of those men of whom nature forms but few, and casts them on our globe perhaps once in a century!"

The new year 1794 was ushered in by a decree from the Convention, ordering the people to celebrate the anniversary of Louis XVI.'s death as a national festival. Then, too, were destroyed the remains of the former kings of France, hitherto so carefully preserved at St. Denis. In carrying out this destruction, many famous historic tombs, priceless works of art, were badly damaged, and valuable relics were stolen or lost. Still, the remains were not so radically disposed of as some supposed, for it is said considerable royal dust was later discovered in these very tombs, which have since been carefully restored.

The Reign of Terror had spread all over France because members of the Convention were sent out, clothed with absolute power, to take charge of affairs in the various provinces. Carrier, for instance, the member who had control in the Vendee, proved a most cruel man, and about this time began executing all captured rebels—men, women, and children. As the guillotine could not work fast enough, he embarked hosts of captives in rotten ships, which he ordered scuttled in the middle of the river Loire. After a while, however, even old ships seemed too precious to sacrifice, so the prisoners, tied in cruel derision in pairs, this was called a Republican marriage,—were thrown overboard, to sink after a few vain efforts to keep afloat. Thus the Loire kept rolling corpses down to the sea for several months, as, all told, in these drownings, Carrier disposed of at least fifteen thousand victims.

Indeed, no one was safe in those days; those who were up to-day were likely to be down to-morrow. Desmoulins, the man who started the Revolution by his speech in the Palais Royal garden, after being a popular favorite for some time, was arrested and sent to the guillotine, heartbroken at the idea of being separated from his beautiful young wife. And, because this unfortunate lady haunted the neighborhood of his prison, in quest of news, she, too, was arrested and executed, a fortnight later. Danton, whose fiery speeches excited the people to invade the Tuileries and massacre the Swiss guards, and who argued for the execution of the king, was further noted as president of the Jacobin Club, and founder of the Revolutionary Tribunal. Although he now began to advocate moderation, his voice was no longer heard; he who had once been leader, having incurred the jealousy of Robespierre, was arrested with Desmoulins and brought to trial, too. When asked, as usual, his name and abode, Danton proudly stated: My name? It is Danton, a name tolerably well known in the Revolution. My dwelling? It will soon be nowhere, but my name will live in the Pantheon of history!" During his trial he stated: "Just one year ago, I was instrumental in instituting the Revolutionary Tribunal; I beg God and men to forgive me." The bloody tribunal which he founded now sentenced him to death (1794), and his last words to the executioner were, "Show the people my head; it is worth seeing!"

Not only were politicians executed, but harmless poets like Chenier, who on the scaffold struck his brow, exclaiming, "I have done naught as yet for posterity, and still, there was something there!" Scientists fared no better. Condorcet, the mathematician, was tracked from one hiding place to another, and would have been guillotined, had not sudden death by apoplexy, or poison, saved him from that fate. The "Founder of Modern Chemistry," Lavoisier, begged for time to leave the world some record of an invaluable discovery he had made, only to be harshly informed by his grossly ignorant judges that "the Republic has no need of scientists!" Thus, as another writer remarked, "It took them only a moment to decree the fall of that head, and still a hundred years perchance will not suffice to produce another like it!" Even the philanthropic physician, Dr. Guillotin—a friend of Franklin, who had persuaded Louis XVI. that it would be more humane to execute criminals by a mechanical device than to rely solely as heretofore upon an executioner's ax and uncertain aim—proved another of the innocent victims of the guillotine, which, although it owes its name to him, was invented by some one else.

Death of Madam Elizabeth

Ever since Marie Antoinette had bidden her daughter and sister-in-law farewell, they had remained in the Temple, where three times a day guards entered their room to bring food, and occasionally appeared to search their rooms for traces of conspiracy, confiscating everything which seemed suspicious. But Madam Elizabeth was such a good and sensible woman, that she comforted her niece and trained her to take the utmost care of the two small rooms they occupied, of her clothes, and of her health. Every day the girl had to exercise during a certain length of time, walking up and down the room, for since the king's death they had never been down in the gardens, and since the queen's removal had even been denied air and exercise on the tower platform.

From time to time the princesses gleaned scanty news of poor little Louis, but what they heard so wrung their hearts that, to divert themselves, they read their few books of devotion over and over, and knitted and sewed diligently, ripping and re-ripping for the sake of an occupation, as new materials were denied them. Madam Elizabeth suspected that Marie Antoinette had been executed; still, as no positive tidings reached her, she would not sadden her little niece by imparting to her such ghastly fears.

One day, with just as little warning as when they came for the queen, men arrived to take Elizabeth away, vouchsafing no answers to her questions. The little princess said afterwards that her aunt urged her to have courage and firmness, to hope always in God, to practice the good principles of religion given her by her parents, and not to fail in the last instructions given her by her father and mother. Madam Elizabeth was immediately summoned before the court, where the worst real charges brought were that she had written to her émigré brothers, and that she had begged to remain with the king and queen in prison! Besides, her judges accused her of all manner of fancied base deeds, declaring that they felt sure she must be plotting mischief, as they could find no trace of her diamonds! She answered patiently at first; then, seeing all efforts were wasted, she exclaimed: "All these questions are, however, useless; you want my life. I have offered up to God the sacrifice of my being, and I am prepared to die, happy at the thought of rejoining my revered brother and his wife, whom I loved so dearly when on earth."

As loyalty to the late king was now high treason, this blameless princess was sentenced to the guillotine, with ten noble ladies and fourteen gentlemen, the judges grimly calling these people "her court," for they frequently indulged in ghastly jokes of that order. Having long been prepared to die, Madam Elizabeth heard her sentence calmly, and spent her few remaining hours comforting and strengthening those who were to be executed with her. To a mother, who wailed that while she felt resigned to die herself, she could not bear the thought of death for her son, aged twenty, Elizabeth said: "You love your son, and yet you do not wish him to accompany you! You are going yourself to the joys of heaven, and you want him to stay upon earth, where all is now torture and sorrow!" In the tumbrel on the way to the scaffold, she cheered her unfortunate companions by saying, "You have shown your compatriots how to live rightly; show them now how men die when their consciences are at peace!"

Hoping to shake the courage of the princess, the executioners decreed that she should be last, but Madam Elizabeth remained perfectly calm, embracing each of the women victims as they went up the steps to the guillotine, and allowing each of the men to take leave of her by kissing her hand, as was then customary in polite society. To the last victim she said firmly, "Courage and faith in God's mercy!" and, when called herself, submitted patiently to the last indignities, exclaiming only when the executioner roughly removed her kerchief, "In the name of your mother, sir, cover me!" Madam Elizabeth was executed in May, 1794, at the age of thirty, and thus little Louis and his sister were the only royal captives left in the gloomy prison, where the "Orphans of the Temple" were, however, never allowed to see each other again.

Death of Robespierre

You have seen how, since the Republic had been declared, even worship had undergone sundry changes. Still, the Goddess of Reason did not long maintain her fantastic sway, and when Hebert, the author of this cult, ceased to be popular, he, too, was guillotined, after being jeered at by the people for the cowardice he displayed. Robespierre, who was now the controlling spirit of the Revolution, carried through a decree that the people should henceforth worship the Supreme Being."

On June 8, therefore, the Parisians assembled on the Field of Mars, to see Robespierre in a sky-blue coat, bearing flowers, fruit, and grain in his hand, officiate as high priest, after announcing, "To-day let us enjoy ourselves, to-morrow begin afresh to fight the enemies of the Republic." His main weapon for fighting French foes was the guillotine, which, for the first time in many months, stood idle for a whole day, shrouded in festive purple hangings! But it was by means of the "Holy Guillotine"—as it was sacrilegiously called—that the Republic now coined money, the property of all victims being confiscated for the benefit of the state. The "Supreme Being" ceremonies, arranged by the painter David, proved very stagy, for they concluded with the public burning of two straw figures, "Atheism" and "Egotism," out of which, at a signal from Robespierre, arose "Wisdom," badly blackened by the smoke!

Robespierre, "more despotic than any Bourbon," proved the most bloodthirsty of all the Revolutionary leaders, for he made such changes in the Revolutionary Tribunal that nearly every prisoner tried was quickly condemned to death. Still, many stories are told of brave and touching deeds, of heroic self-sacrifice, and of narrow escapes, which you will read in more detailed books. One aged couple so touched even a Revolutionary judge, that he tried hard to save them from the knife by distorting facts. But the old gentleman, too honorable to tell a lie or to permit one to be told in his behalf, frustrated this charitable impulse by proclaiming: "I thank you for the efforts you have made to save us, but we could never redeem our lives by a falsehood. My wife and I prefer to die. We have grown old together without having ever told a falsehood, and we will not lie now, not even to save a remnant of life. Do your duty as we are doing ours. We will not blame you, but the law only, for our death."

Many of the men showed the white feather at the last moment, but among all the delicate, aristocratic women who were executed, not one failed to maintain her womanly dignity to the very end. In fact, the only woman who made a great fuss—crying, screaming, and falling at the feet of judges and executioners—was Madame du Barry, the last favorite of Louis XV. She had been one of the first to escape from France, but had returned in disguise to recover jewels and plate which she had buried in her garden. In her hasty flight from France, it seems that this lady had cruelly deserted a colored dwarf slave, of whom she had made such a pet that he figures in most of the paintings representing this wicked yet beautiful woman. The dwarf so deeply resented this treatment that, on recognizing his former mistress in her disguise, he went and denounced her to the Revolutionary Tribunal, revenging himself by thus compassing her death.

The government by the Convention and the Committee of Public Safety had one good result: the French armies were made strong enough to drive back the allied invaders, and even to carry the war beyond the borders of France. But about one month after winning the battle of Fleurus (1794), the Convention, feeling it could no longer stand Robespierre's tyranny, had him arrested with his brother and principal helpers. In the Convention Robespierre argued and defended himself, until he fairly choked, when a man in the background cried out tauntingly, "It is the blood of Danton which chokes you!" This tragic reminder of the way in which Robespierre had abandoned a former ally, decided his fate. Robespierre and his companions, who had condemned so many to die, showed far less courage than many of their victims, and several tried to commit suicide in various ways; indeed, Robespierre's lower jaw being fractured by a pistol shot, he had to appear before his judges on a stretcher.

After a very brief trial, Robespierre and his adherents were condemned to the guillotine, where Robespierre died shrieking, owing to the pain in his broken jaw when the bandage was removed (July, 1794). When he was executed, the spectators clapped loudly, for they were glad to be rid of him. There were always many people present at executions; indeed, throughout the Revolution, executions served as an entertainment, attracting large audiences, the front seats being always claimed by the lowest class of women, known as "the Knitters" *(les tricoteuses)* because they knitted industriously while eagerly watching all that was going on. Over Robespierre's grave was found one day the following inscription, expressing a great deal of truth:—

> "Lament not, that I lie in my last bed,
> For, were I living, friend, you would be dead."

The death of Robespierre marks the end of the Reign of Terror in Paris, during which nearly 3000 persons had been guillotined. Still, the massacres could not immediately be stopped, so in the course of the next two days the guillotine worked as hard as ever. But, after that, prisons were opened, 20,000 captives set free, fewer arrests made, and soon no sentences of death were issued save in case of real criminals,—such, for instance, as Carrier, of "drowning" fame; Simon, the tutor of the poor little Dauphin; and the cruel judge of the Revolutionary Tribunal (Fouquier-Tinville).

Among the persons who would have died within the next few days, had Robespierre lived, was Josephine, who was to be the first Empress of France.

The clubs where Marat, Danton, Robespierre, and others had excited each other to such frightful deeds of violence, were ordered closed, and "the Gilded Youth," a political party in favor of greater moderation, now began to make its presence felt. Still, the *Red* Reign of Terror, so fortunately ended, was offset by a *White* Reign of Terror in the southeast, where Royalists took their revenge by murdering many Revolutionists, these massacres continuing more than six months before they could be effectually checked.

End of the Revolution

Years of trouble and horror had passed, but the year 1795 was fortunately to bring brighter days to France. At its very beginning, the Republican armies entered Holland, where, undaunted by the extreme cold, French soldiers made themselves masters of the country, and of its fleets, held fast by the ice in the Zuider Zee. Thus, you see, a mere detachment of cavalry could master the dauntless Dutch navy! The French were so anxious to have every one follow the example they were giving to the world, that they presently induced the Dutch to send away their stadtholder, and to organize into a new state, known during its brief existence as the Batavian Republic.

The triumphs of the French Republican army, whose glorious record was eight pitched battles, 116 towns and 230 forts taken, 90,000 prisoners, and 3800 cannon captured, so awed all Europe, that Prussia and Spain made peace with France. Proud as the nation was of these successes, lack of bread still caused constant rioting, and once a mob even burst into the hall where the Convention was sitting, to clamor for food. In the confusion, one rioter aimed a shot at the president, and killed the deputy who bravely flung himself in the way. When the head of this hero was brought before the president, on a pike, a few moments later, he gravely and respectfully saluted it, saying boldly it was "the head of a brave man," whereupon the fickle mob, suddenly agreeing with him, honored their own victim with a grand funeral.

Before the Convention closed (Oct. 26, 1795), a new government was provided, which was to consist of a Council of Ancients and one of Five Hundred, together with a board of five Directors. As you have seen, the Convention had issued some very wise and some very foolish and wicked decrees during the three years and more of its sway. Its attitude toward religion had changed from time to time. In the end it decreed religious liberty, but provided that the government should not pay the expenses of any form of worship. One of its last acts was to provide that the square where the guillotine had stood (pages 90, 91) should henceforth be known as Place de la Concorde (or Harmony Square)!

Just before the Convention disbanded, violent riots again broke out, and it became evident that the palace of the Tuileries—now used for the government of the Republic—would again be stormed. Barras, whose voice was now heard most often, suggested armed resistance, and when the objection was made that most of the officers sympathized too keenly with the Parisians to be trusted, he exclaimed, "I have the very man you want; he is a little Corsican officer who will not stand upon ceremony." This "little Corsican officer" was Napoleon Bonaparte, who, since the siege of Toulon, had been both idle and unhappy, and so poor that he had to pawn his watch to secure six-cent dinners. When asked at the present juncture whether he felt competent to defend the Convention, Bonaparte answered boldly, "Perfectly, and I am in the habit of accomplishing what I undertake!" This answer pleased the authorities, who gave him full powers, thus enabling Bonaparte, in the course of the next night, to place his cannon so that he could sweep with grapeshot every street leading up to the palace.

Early the next morning, the Parisians came—an army 40,000 strong—to invade the Tuileries. After allowing them to draw sufficiently near, Bonaparte, without the least compunction, gave orders to fire, and, as he had predicted when the mob invaded the Tuileries in the days of Louis XVI., the death of a few hundred men so terrified the rest that all fled. Bonaparte thus kept his promise, winning such prestige by this triumph that he was able shortly after to disarm the Parisians, who ever since the taking of the Bastille had been well armed, and hence able to take an active part in every fray.

With the grapeshot which quelled the rioters, Bonaparte also put an end to the Revolution, of which the greatest permanent effect was the establishment of civil and religious equality in the eyes of the law. As already mentioned, the Revolution also caused the adoption of the metric system of weights and measures, a system which has been of lasting advantage to the country; but the Convention's attempt to revise the calendar proved an utter failure, although it was given a fair trial of over ten years. This plan was to begin numbering the years from September 21, 1792, which was called "the

Republican Era." Each year was to contain twelve months of thirty days; the five days extra in ordinary years—and six in leap years—were to be devoted to national festivals, dedicated to Genius, Industry, Fine Actions, Rewards, and Public Opinion, and were dubbed collectively "Sansculottide Days." The old month names were replaced by the "vintage," "mist," and "frost "months for autumn; the "snow," "rain," and "wind "months for winter; the "bud," "flower," and "meadow "months for spring; and the "harvest," "heat," and "fruit "months for summer *(vendemiaire, brumaire, frirnaire; nivose, pluviose, ventose; germinal, floreal, prairial; messidor, thermidor, fructidor)*. The week was abolished; instead, the month was divided into "decades "of ten days each, the last day of each decade being set aside for rest.

It is estimated that the French Revolution cost France about 1,000,000 lives, many of those who perished being the elite (choice) of the nation. But, strange to relate, all the riots and massacres of these six years seemed to effect little change in the daily life of the people, which went on much as usual. Some people even invented new styles of dress called "victim fashions" *(a la victime)* and wore miniature guillotines as ornaments, many of them having apparently assumed the old motto, "Let us eat, drink, and be merry, for tomorrow we die!"

The Orphans of the Temple

It was on June 8, 1795, before the Convention finished its sessions, that another of the Temple prisoners left its walls forever. That was little Louis Capet, once the Dauphin, and since his father's death known by Royalists as Louis XVII., although he never reigned. You remember that this poor child entered the Temple in August, 1792, and that about a year later, after his father's death, he was torn from his mother to be intrusted to the brutal care of Simon. Now, it is believed that some of the rabid Revolutionists, feeling that they *could not* guillotine a child, and not daring to get rid of him by secret assassination lest they be found out, wished to undermine his health by confinement and ill treatment, so he would die a natural death, thus putting a stop to all Royalist attempts to place him on his father's throne.

The brutal Simon had the care of this innocent victim until Madam Elizabeth was removed from the Temple. Shortly after that, Madam Royal heard a great commotion, and fancied that her little brother was being removed to another place. The men who brought her scanty meals (they themselves now ate the food intended for the royal prisoners), and those who, three times a day and sometimes in the middle of the night, suddenly entered and searched her room to discover whether she could be corresponding with "traitors," answered all her questions by saying only, "I advise you to have patience and to trust in the justice and goodness of Frenchmen."

The noise which had prompted Madam Royal's vain questions was caused by the moving of Simon and of his wife,—now tired of prison life,—and by the transfer of her poor little brother to a room upstairs, where, young as he was, his jailers were going to leave him many months all alone. Only once during all that time was Louis's room cleaned, and it was never aired, the window being covered and nailed fast to insure safety. The child's food was handed to him through a wicket, where he was obliged to show his face night or day, whenever called by the men on guard, and the only light he saw at night was that flashed on his pale features by the sentinel's lantern!

Poor little Louis was so afraid of every one by this time, that he never dared speak to the sentinels, and, during the last months of his captivity, he proved so dumb that a few of the men actually believed a deaf-mute child had been locked up there instead of the little prince! This suspicion gave rise to many romantic stories, in which the prince is said to have escaped, and to have lived to grow up, marry, and have children, whose descendants still exist.

Every day the small prisoner was given a crock of water, so he could have washed and kept clean, and he had a broom with which he might have swept his room, yet he did nothing of the sort, simply because he had always been washed, dressed, and waited upon, and was not accustomed to do anything for himself. Without books, or toys, or other means of occupation, amusement, or exercise, the child naturally became dull and listless, and the uncleanliness and bad air so undermined his health, that when he was finally given a bath and clean clothes, and later placed in another room with an attendant as kind as he dared be to this pitiful wreck, it was only too evident that the child had only a short time to live.

Then, Robespierre being dead, at last, the government, more humanely inclined, sent to the little patient a doctor who had attended him in his happy days, but now could do naught but ease his last moments. Even then the poor boy still remembered his mother, for he once piteously begged to go to her, ceasing only when told that such a request would endanger his kind keeper's life. Although Louis now had company by day, he was still always locked up alone at night, and although the sister who had been his beloved playmate was under the selfsame roof, he was never allowed one glimpse of her face!

We are told that he suffered greatly from tumors and sores,—the result of neglect and harsh treatment,—but that he was always patient and gentle. Once, when his attendant expressed regret at his anguish, the poor little laddie said, "Console yourself; I shall not suffer always." No, the poor little martyr's trials were nearly over. A few moments before he died, a smile—the first in many months—passed over his wasted face as with a rapturous look he exclaimed that he heard his mother singing! A moment later his spirit had left the place where he had been so unhappy, and had gone to join that of his beloved parents. Louis XVII. was then ten years and two months old (1795), having spent nearly three years of this short life in the Temple prison.

A few months later, just when the Convention was drawing to a close, his sister, who had been alone in her prison ever since Madam Elizabeth's departure, was allowed the company of a woman, and was soon after informed that she would be sent to Austria, in exchange for the commissioners surrendered by Dumouriez. But it was only a few hours before she left the Temple, that her eager questions were finally answered and she was told in the briefest and baldest way that she no longer had mother, brother, or aunt! When the death of her aunt was made known to her, Madam Royal exclaimed in broken-hearted accents: "What! Elizabeth, too! She was a saint!"

Do you wonder that this poor girl had written on her prison walls: "Marie Therese is the most unhappy creature in the world. She can obtain no news of her mother, nor be reunited to her, though she has asked it a thousand times!" But after the above news had been communicated to her, she traced the words, "Oh, my God! forgive those who have made my family die," thus proving that she, like her brother, was mindful of the last injunctions of her parents.

This poor young princess left her awful prison where she had been three and a half years, on her seventeenth birthday, to be escorted to the Austrian frontier, where she was exchanged for the other prisoners. From Vienna, at her request, she was sent to Russia to join her uncle (her father's brother, the "clever boy"), who, ever since her little brother's death, had claimed the empty title of Louis XVIII., King of France. In 1799, four years after leaving prison, she married the Duke of Angouleme, eldest son of her father's second brother (Count of Artois), as had already been decided in the happy days of her childhood, so you will hear of her again, as Duchess of Angouleme, for she was to play a further part in French history.

The Youth of Napoleon

The new government, called "the Directory," which was to last four years (1795-1799), was organized under the "Constitution of the Year III." Under this plan, the lawmaking power was given, as we have seen, to two assemblies—that of the Five Hundred, which proposed measures, and that of the Ancients, which ratified or rejected them; and the executive power was intrusted to five Directors. The men first chosen as Directors were Carnot, Barras, and three other Republicans, who immediately proceeded to establish themselves in the Luxembourg, the beautiful palace built by the widow of Henry IV. But, while they found there magnificently decorated ceilings and walls, and superb hardwood floors, not an article of furniture was left, so they had to borrow a rickety pine table and a few straw-bottom chairs from the janitor to use in their first meeting.

The new government promised so many good things that the people, anxious to forget the grim past, looked gayly forward toward the future. A great reaction had set in after all the terror and gloom of the past few years, and need was felt for brightness and gayety of all kinds. As a rule, it is those in the highest places who set the fashion, and as the most influential of the Directors was Barras,—a man of bad principles, who loved show and diversion,—it became the rage to dress extravagantly, as he did, and to indulge in all manner of pleasures. Some of these were innocent enough, but people who prided themselves upon having no religion did not know exactly where to stop.

Barras, who was a great admirer of beauty and wit, liked to collect in his drawing-room all the most clever men and most charming women. Among the ladies frequently seen at his receptions were Madame Tallien, a noted beauty; Josephine de Beauharnais, whose husband had been guillotined and who had barely escaped the same fate; and Madame Recamier, whose grace and beauty were proverbial. These ladies affected a Greek style of dress, with very short waist, which, from the time when it appeared in France, has always been known as the "Directoire" or "Empire" fashion. Among the many interesting men was Bonaparte, "the little Corsican officer," who now had a chance to see Josephine, with whom he fell desperately in love. He was, howev-

Napoleon During His Youth

er, quite as poor as she, and as there were two Beauharnais children to support, marriage seemed almost impossible. Still, Josephine was so fascinating, and such a favorite with Barras, that she confidently believed a way would open for this young officer before long.

Josephine was right, for Carnot, who had ably looked after the Republican armies for many years, was making an elaborate plan for attacking Austria and Germany, with which the Republic was still at war. By this plan, three armies were to start from different points, two in the north and one in the south, to meet later at Vienna, and bring the Emperor to terms. As two of the Directors, Carnot and Barras, had already seen what Bonaparte could do, they gave this young man, then twenty-seven, the command of the southern army, at Josephine's request.

A few days, therefore, before Bonaparte's departure to join the army and show what he could do, he and Josephine were married, "Republican fashion"; that is to say, without any religious ceremony whatever. As these two persons are to be often mentioned hereafter, you will be interested in hearing about the early life of each of them.

Napoleon Bonaparte was the second of ten children, and, although both his parents were Italian, he always claimed to be French, because he was born in Corsica a short time after that island was united to France. Father Bonaparte, though a poor officer, educated these children as best he could, sending Napoleon to Brienne, a preparatory military school, at the age of ten.

Napoleon was, from childhood, extremely obstinate and intensely vain. It hurt his feelings so sorely to be less well dressed than the other boys, that he proved gloomy and reserved at first, refusing to mix with the other pupils or to make friends. After a while, however, he began to shine in mathematics and in games, especially in those where he could direct the motions of others and act as leader, his side being always sure to win in snowball fights, for instance. While at Brienne, Napoleon lost his father, who, in the midst of his wildest delirium, is said to have uttered these prophetic words: "Where is my son, Napoleon? He whose sword will make kings tremble, he who will change the face of the world!" After remaining five years at Brienne, the boy about whom such great deeds were foretold, was transferred to the military academy in Paris, bearing a note from his former teachers, saying, "He will do great things if fortune favors him."

Graduating from this school as second lieutenant of artillery, Bonaparte was stationed in various garrisons in southern France, where, having nothing save his pay—generally in arrears—and hence not being able to lead or shine in military circles, he became retiring and gloomy, read a great deal, and even tried to write an immortal novel. At the siege of Toulon, he got his first chance to distinguish himself, and attracted the attention of Barras, but afterwards, the government having meantime changed, Bonaparte was imprisoned for a while. When he returned to Paris, he was out of both work and money, and, in answer to his applications for an appointment, received everywhere the discouraging reply, "You are too young," although he vehemently urged, "One ages fast on the battlefield!" while proudly mentioning his previous services.

Just as Bonaparte, in despair, was about to offer his services to Turkey, Barras called upon him, as we have seen, to subdue the Parisians; and shortly after the Directory had been instituted, he was appointed general in chief of the army destined to invade Italy.

Josephine, being born of French parents in the West Indies, was often called a Creole (a name applied to European children born in the tropics). She came to France, very young, to marry Viscount de Beauharnais, and they had two children, Eugene and Hortense, of whom you will hear more. The Beauharnais couple having quarreled, Josephine returned to her parents with her little daughter, but the dispute was patched up by letters, so that she returned once more to France. She was then so poor that her little girl, having worn out her only pair of shoes in dancing to amuse the sailors, gladly accepted from one of them a pair of slippers rudely cobbled from the tops of an old pair of boots!

When the Revolution broke out, the Beauharnais couple, being aristocrats, became "suspects" and were put in prison, their children being barely kept alive by the devotion of an old servant, who had to bind them out as apprentices. As you have seen, Beauharnais was guillotined, and Josephine escaped a similar fate by Robespierre's fall. Just after Bonaparte had turned his cannon on the Parisians, he ordered all the houses searches for weapons, which were to be deposited once more in the city arsenals. In this search, the sword of Beauharnais, which hung in Eugene's room, and which he considered his most precious treasure, was ruthlessly carried off. Hoping to recover it, the lad hastened to headquarters, where he pleaded so eloquently that Bonaparte gave it back. The next day, Josephine came with her son to thank the general, and the acquaintance thus begun soon ripened into love and marriage. Although the Bonaparte honeymoon proved very short, the bridegroom was desperately in love, for he wrote letters to his beloved bride at every relay, while posting southward to join his forces.

Bonaparte in Italy

When Bonaparte reached the army, early in 1796, he found he was none too welcome to the officers, all of whom were older, had served longer, and therefore thought themselves better fitted for the post of command. Besides, the new general was then thin and sallow, and owing to his small stature looked far more like a boy than a great man. At the first council, however, where he boldly differed in opinion from all the rest, he made his authority so well felt that one of his subordinates exclaimed, after he left them, "Gentlemen, we have found our master!"

The task which Bonaparte was thus undertaking was not easy, for his forces were only about half as large as those he was called to combat; there was no money for campaign expenses, and the soldiers, hungry, ragged, and badly shod, were half disposed to rebel, as they had not received any pay for a long time. Still, in his very first speech, Bonaparte changed their sullen apathy into wild enthusiasm, for, knowing "that imagination governs minds," he spoke as follows: "Soldiers, you are poorly fed and almost naked. The government owes you much, but can do nothing. I am about to lead you into the most fertile country in the world. There, great cities and prosperous provinces await you. There, you will find honor, glory, and riches. Soldiers of the army of Italy, will you lack courage for the enterprise?"

This recognition of their grievances, and strong appeal to all their passions—to the highest as well as to the lowest—so fired the soldiers that they set out full of courage and ambition, along the old Roman shore road, and soon crossed the Alps by a low pass insufficiently guarded by the enemy. In

Italy they had to meet both the Sardinian and the Austrian forces, which Bonaparte was thus able to fight singly. He skillfully separated them by winning several small battles. Then, having advanced within a few miles of Turin, the capital of the kingdom of Sardinia, he received the messengers who came to bargain for peace, with the haughty retort: "Terms? It is I who name the terms. Accept them at once, or Turin will be in my hands to-morrow!"

The terrified Sardinians promptly made a treaty (Cherasco) and withdrew from the war, thus leaving Bonaparte free to accomplish the second and more difficult part of his task. Once more the soldiers were spurred on by one of his "volcanic" speeches, in which he began by artfully praising them for what they had done, saying: "Soldiers, you have won in a fortnight six victories, taken twenty-one flags, fifty-five cannon, several fortresses, and conquered the richest part of Piedmont! You have taken fifteen thousand prisoners, killed or wounded more than ten thousand men! You have won battles without cannon, crossed rivers without bridges, made forced marches without shoes, camped without rum and often without bread. The Republican phalanxes, the soldiers of Liberty, were alone capable of undergoing what you have undergone! Thanks be to you for it. But, soldiers, you have done nothing yet, since there still remains work for you to do."

Thus stimulated, and full of the generous enthusiasm which soldiers always feel for a general who enables them to triumph, even by dint of extra efforts, the French bravely met the Austrians at Lodi, where general and men, swept on by the same brave impulse, forced their way over a bridge to reach the foe beyond. It was here that Bonaparte earned his proudest title, "the Little Corporal," his men declaring he had marched side by side with them, just as if he had been nothing more than a petty officer. One who witnessed this thrilling charge wrote in regard to it: "It was strange to see him, on that bridge of Lodi, mixed up with his tall grenadiers. He looked a mere boy!" Those tall grenadiers, by the way, were Bonaparte's special pets, and whenever he was particularly pleased with one of them, he was wont to show his satisfaction by reaching up the full length of his arm, and playfully tweaking the giant's ear! These men called him "Gray-coat" (la Redingote Grise), because he often wore a long gray overcoat.

The soldiers devotion was due largely to Bonaparte's care for their comfort and to the sympathetic view he took of some of their shortcomings. We are informed, for instance, that once during this Italian campaign a sentinel, who had fallen asleep on duty, suddenly woke up to see his general, musket in hand, mounting guard in his stead. But all Bonaparte said to the delinquent on this occasion was: "My friend, here is your musket. You have fought hard and marched long, so your slumber is excusable. But the army might be lost by a moment's inattention. I happened to be awake and have held your post for you. You will be more careful hereafter, I know."

End of the Italian War

After the victory of Lodi, Bonaparte soon drove the Austrian army out of Milan, which he entered in triumph. Austria then sent army after army against him, each larger than his own, but he attacked them unexpectedly and defeated them all, in three great battles. The last of these in 1796 was at Arcole, where seeing his men hesitate to cross a bridge,—swept like that at Lodi by the enemy's cannon,—Bonaparte quickly seized one of the red, white, and blue Republican flags, and, dashing ahead, led them on to victory.

These repeated triumphs were meantime filling the hearts of the French people with pride and joy, and those of the enemy with rage and fear. Many hesitated to measure their strength against so able a foe, among others the Duke of Parma, the Duke of Modena, and the Pope, all three of whom compromised and made treaties with France. As one city after another opened its gates to Bonaparte, the Austrians were forced to retreat in dismay, leaving him free to besiege Mantua, their greatest stronghold in Italy. Meanwhile the two northern armies, under Jourdan and Moreau, were working hard, too. Moreau swept on victorious, until not very far from Vienna; but the other general, less fortunate, met defeat and was driven back, while Bonaparte was not yet ready to advance beyond Italy. Moreau, therefore, left alone to cope with the enemy in his own land, beat a masterly retreat without losing a cannon or a man. The Austrians, encouraged by these northern triumphs, and further aided by sundry rebellions in Italian cities, now sent greater forces against Bonaparte, who seemed, at last, to be caught fast in their toils. When he therefore ordered a retreat, his men obeyed in sullen silence, but when the soldiers perceived that this move was a mere feint which would enable them to win another triumph, they fought with such ardor that they won a brilliant victory at Rivoli, early in 1797. About one month later, Mantua—in which one of the Austrian armies had taken refuge—was forced to surrender, and the French army then pushed on into Austria, until halted by offers of peace.

After long negotiations, the famous treaty of Campo Formio was agreed upon; by this, France was to have Belgium, with the Rhine as northern frontier, and to remain in possession of Savoy, Nice, and some other conquests; northern Italy was to form the Cisalpine Republic, the Pope losing some of his territory; and Venice,—including Dalmatia, Istria, and much of northeastern Italy,—after nearly fourteen centuries of independence, was to belong to Austria. Once, in the course of these discussions, when the Austrian plenipotentiary (a man armed with full powers) refused to grant certain conditions, Bonaparte in a rage suddenly dashed a precious vase to pieces on the floor, crying, "I will break your monarchy as I have broken this!" This savage threat had the desired effect, as did also the haughty boast, "The Republic is like the sun; only the blind fail to recognize it!" when objection was made to acknowledging the change of government in France.

Napoleon Victorious at the Battle of Rivoli

The peace secured by Bonaparte, so gratifying in many respects, was a great disappointment to General Hoche (Osh), who, having finished the long war in the vendee, had hastened on to join the northern armies. He won several battles, and was about to capture an Austrian army when the peace was made. But, although Hoche promised to be a worthy rival of Bonaparte, his career was cut short by an early death.

Meantime, Bonaparte had all along been carrying out the program he had made in the beginning, plundering ruthlessly everywhere. Not only did he obtain millions enough, as booty and tribute, to supply all the needs of his army and to send money to the government at home, but he wrung from each city its choicest art treasures, which were immediately forwarded to France. In this way the Louvre owned at one time nearly all the great masterpieces of Europe, most of which, however, France was obliged to restore to their owners a few years later, as we shall see.

Bonaparte, who had left Paris poor, lived now in Italy like a prince, his wife and family having joined him to enjoy his triumphs and to share in his good fortune. But nevertheless, he was closely watching matters in Paris and elsewhere, for he had now fully made up his mind to become master, and, as he expressed it, was "only waiting until the pear was ripe." He knew "the pear" was beginning to ripen, because the Directory was having the utmost difficulty to hold its own.

The people were so discontented with this government that in 1797 they elected many Royalist members of the Councils; but soon after, by a *coup d'etat,*—a sudden seizure of power, or forcible change in government,—three of the Directors deposed the other two, and excluded the Royalist members from the Councils. The feeling of unrest spread beyond the French frontiers. Switzerland, adopting French Republican ideas, and being aided by French troops, overthrew its old government and replaced it with a new one, taking the name of Helvetian Republic. Before long, six such little republics were established in Europe, for, besides the Batavian, Helvetian, and Cisalpine republics already mentioned, the French helped in the formation of the Ligurian Republic in Genoa, the Roman in Rome, and the Parthenopean in Naples— by stirring up trouble in these places by underhand means, and then interfering openly under pretext of quelling disturbances and restoring order!

Just as 1797 was drawing to a close, Bonaparte returned to Paris to receive the plaudits of a grateful people when he publicly deposited the treaty of Campo Formio on the altar of his country. Talleyrand who was to be first his friend and later his foe embraced him publicly on that occasion, hailing him as "the man of the centuries," while Bonaparte, not to be outdone in fine-sounding phrases, spoke of France as "the Great Nation."

The name of the street where Bonaparte lived was changed in his honor to Victory Street, and he was cheered whenever he appeared in the theater; but, for all that, he fully realized that his fame would soon die out unless he did something to keep himself before the eyes and mind of the public. Seeing that the time was not yet ripe to change the government to his advantage, and that the invasion of England, which the Directory proposed, was not feasible,—owing principally to the fact that there were not enough French ships to transport the required armed forces across the Channel,—Bonaparte suggested attacking England in her colonies, saying that by depriving her of her Indian Empire, she would be robbed of her chief source of wealth, and hence of "sinews" for her wars.

Expedition to Egypt

When Bonaparte proposed to the Directors to conquer Egypt, and thus prevent the English from reaching India save by way of the Cape of Good Hope, his proposal was accepted—principally because the Directors were jealous of his success and popularity, and desperately afraid lest he should not only eclipse, but, in time, supplant them. Preparations were therefore hastened, and he sailed from Toulon in May, 1798, with a force of tried soldiers and fine officers.

The English, warned of the preparation of the French fleet, but not knowing its destination, sent ships to re-enforce their admiral Nelson, near Toulon, so that he could fight it. These ships arrived too late, and Nelson cruised wildly around the Mediterranean, trying to find the French fleet. Meantime, Bonaparte had stopped at Malta, where, under pretext of renewing his fresh water supply, he landed some of his troops. Then, as had been previously arranged, traitors threw open the gates, thus surrendering to the French, without a blow, the mighty fortress which had been the stronghold of the

Knights Hospitalers ever since 1530. But such was the strength of these island defenses, that one of the generals, after examining them, exclaimed, "It was very lucky for us that there was some one inside to open the gates to admit us!"

On the way from Malta to Alexandria, Bonaparte and his staff spent long evenings on deck, enjoying the balmy air, blue seas, and starry skies. Once, when one of the officers expressed atheistic views,—such as were fashionable since the Roman Catholic religion had suffered an eclipse in France,—he was silenced by Bonaparte's pointing to the heavens above them and remarking, "You may talk as much as you please, gentlemen, but tell me who made all that?"

On nearing Alexandria, the French admiral wished to wait a few days to effect a safer landing; but Bonaparte, knowing that time was precious and that he must land before the English could come up to prevent it, insisted upon disembarking immediately. He soon became master of the city of Alexandria, and then, while the navy moved off to anchor at Abukir, he set out to march with the army to Cairo. On the way thither, perceiving that new conditions required new methods, Bonaparte arranged that at any alarm his troops should form in squares, placing their baggage, laden on donkeys, and all noncombatants in the center. As his expedition was accompanied by a corps of illustrious scientists,—to study the country and its resources, and to select its choicest treasures to ship back to France as trophies,—the usual cry, when any danger threatened, was, "Form square, donkeys and scientists to the center!"

It was within sight of the hoary Pyramids that Bonaparte first encountered the fierce Mamelukes who were then the ruling class in Egypt. He gave the signal for battle, with the brief reminder, "Soldiers, from the summits of those Pyramids forty centuries are looking down upon you!" Here the foe were so sorely beaten that all Egypt was practically conquered, and Bonaparte could enter Cairo without striking another blow. Then, while one of his generals pursued the fleeing Mamelukes as far as the Nile cataracts, Bonaparte busied himself and his corps of scientists in ascertaining the resources of the country so as to increase its productivity. He also ordered many of the ancient canals repaired, and planned a Suez Canal (not constructed till after his time). He respected the native customs and beliefs; ate lentils like the inhabitants; took part in the Nile festival,—at the time when the flood begins,—where he was called "favorite of Allah"; and appeared, we are told, in the native dress.

While Bonaparte was thus busy on land, the French fleet, riding at anchor in Abukir Bay, was discovered by the searching Nelson, who destroyed it in the famous "Battle of the Nile." It was during this battle that the ten-year-old son of Admiral Casabianca proved his obedience to his father's orders by standing "on the burning deck" of the *Orient* until that vessel exploded. Should you not happen to remember this familiar episode, do read it in the poem by Mrs. Hemans.

Bonaparte Before the Sphinx - Jean-Léon Gérôme

On hearing of this naval disaster, Bonaparte exclaimed philosophically, "To France the Fates have decreed the empire of the land—to England that of the sea!" Nevertheless, he knew that this defeat would prevent his receiving supplies or even news from France, and would cut off all present chance of returning thither with his army. He therefore declared, "This reverse will compel us to do even greater things than we had planned," and prepared to cross the Isthmus of Suez and enter Syria, intending to gain the key to the East by becoming master of the fortress of Acre.

On the way to Acre, Bonaparte seized Jaffa, where he ordered a cruel massacre of the Turkish prisoners; and he would have secured the fortress he coveted, had not Sir Sidney Smith come with his fleet to help the Turks defend it. Later Bonaparte declared, "That man marred my destiny!" thinking that the possession of Acre would have enabled him to get the better of both the Turks and the English, their allies. Meantime, a plague had broken out in Bonaparte's army, so that his soldiers were panic-stricken. To hearten them by, proving that the plague was not contagious, Bonaparte went among the sick, even touching those who were most seriously affected by the disease.

Shortly after, forced to retreat to Egypt, and so closely pursued that he could not remove some hopelessly sick men from Jaffa, Bonaparte proposed to the doctor to give them a dose which would hasten their end and prevent their falling into the foe's hands while still alive. This doctor, even under such conditions, proved mindful only of his oath, for he coldly replied, "My art teaches me to cure men, not to kill them."

A host of Turks soon landed at Abukir Bay, with the intention of crushing Bonaparte and his forces. But, instead of accomplishing this purpose, they were themselves destroyed, so that Bonaparte's rule in Egypt was secure.

79

Murat, the friend and future brother-in-law of Bonaparte, distinguished himself in this battle of Abukir by making a brilliant charge at the head of the cavalry. But before this battle could "decide the fate of the world," as Bonaparte said, it had to become known in France, where no news had been received of the Egyptian expedition for so many months, that the Directory felt sure that Bonaparte's bones must already be whitening on the desert sands!

Bonaparte's Coup d'etat

Bonaparte had been without news from home for ten long months, so he was not aware of many important events that happened since his departure. The Directory had governed weakly and unfairly at home, and abroad had so mismanaged things that the recent French conquests in Italy were already lost. The new southern republics, after a brief existence, had been overthrown, and the old governments restored; besides, measures were even now being taken to punish the French, who had robbed Italy so ruthlessly of many treasures, and had detained Pope Pius VI. in captivity! Of course, the news of all these disasters to France delighted her English foes; and Sir Sidney Smith, thinking it might discourage French soldiers so far away from home, sent a bundle of newspapers to Bonaparte. You can imagine how eagerly these newspapers were devoured, but they produced a very different effect from that which was expected.

The French army could not leave, for English vessels were patrolling the Mediterranean, but Bonaparte calculated that one vessel might, perchance, slip through unseen. He therefore left General Kleber in charge of the army in Egypt, and, taking the ablest officers with him, embarked to run the blockade. Some authorities state that Napoleon was only too glad to leave Egypt just after winning a famous victory, because he foresaw that thereafter things would go wrong, and wanted some one else to bear the blame! However that may be, Kleber did not make friends with the Mohammedans, nor did he maintain good order; after sundry ups and downs, he was stabbed from behind, his successor was defeated by an English army, and Egypt was lost to the French.

Meantime, Bonaparte's ship—by great good fortune, and thanks to a heavy fog—passed unseen through the English blockade, so he could land in France, to announce his Egyptian triumphs, which lost nothing by his telling! The French, who love glory and success, now remembered that while Bonaparte was at the head of the army, they had been victorious, and that money had been plentiful. They naturally concluded that the Directors and other generals were less capable than Bonaparte, who really felt pleased that things had gone wrong, for he confessed later, "In order that I should become master of France, it was necessary that the Directory should experience reverses during my absence."

These reverses having come, Bonaparte, standing once more before the Directors, chided them like naughty schoolboys, saying: "What have you done with the France I left so glorious? I left peace, I find war; I left you victories, I find defeats; I left you millions, I find starvation!" Then, the pear being "ripe," and therefore ready to pluck, he cleverly laid plans to overthrow the government, by a *coup d'etat* on November 9 (or 18th Brumaire), 1799. Among those who plotted with him were his brother Lucien Bonaparte, president of the Council of Five Hundred; many members of the Council of Ancients; and Sieyes, now one of the Directors. The Directors having been either cowed or induced to resign, both councils were transferred to St. Cloud, where they were closely guarded by soldiers, under pretext of threatened trouble among the people. Thus Bonaparte prepared everything to gain his own way, before marching into the Hall where the Council of Ancients were sitting. They made no opposition whatever to his demands, which were that he and his friends should be empowered to draw up a new constitution. He said: "We want a Republic, founded on true liberty and national representation. We shall have it, I swear. I swear in my own name and in that of my companions in arms!"

On his way to the Hall of the Five Hundred, which he meant to visit next, Bonaparte met one of his military friends, who exclaimed in dismay and anger, "You've gotten yourself in a pretty mess!" But Bonaparte promptly answered: "It was worse at Arcole. Just keep quiet. In half an hour things will change!" Escorted by a few grenadiers, he then marched into the hall of the Five Hundred, which he had no right to enter thus; so the loud, angry cry immediately arose: What is this? Swords here! Armed men! Away! We will have no dictator!" In fact, the indignant roar became so persistent that Bonaparte could not make himself heard. Then one man sprang forward to stab him; whereupon the general turned ghastly pale, lost his presence of mind, and had to be almost carried out of the assembly by his tall grenadiers.

At the door, Bonaparte encountered his brother Lucien, to whom he cried in consternation, "They are going to outlaw me!"

"Outlaw you?" retorted Lucien. "Turn them out of the Hall!" This suggestion was promptly carried out, and the Five Hundred fled in confusion, when the grenadiers charged in with lowered bayonets, after proclaiming at the open door: "In the name of General Bonaparte, this Legislative Assembly is dissolved. Let all good citizens therefore retire!"

This proved the end of the Directory and the beginning of a new government called "the Consulate," Bonaparte and a few helpers directing everything until they could frame a new constitution (the fourth since 1789) and get the people to adopt it. But the proposed changes immediately raised suspicions in the breasts of some of the French, who feared for their hard-won liberties and dreaded a second Cromwell. These fears were, however, quieted for a while by Lucien's theatrical announcement, as he brandished his sword: "For my own part, I swear to run this through my own brother, if he ever strikes a blow at the liberties of the French!"

Nevertheless, the *"liberties* of the French" were already in a bad way. The Revolution, which had culminated in 1794, gave the people the power to control the government by frequent elections; but the Directory had not worked well, and now the people were ready to resign some of their power in order to secure a stronger government. By beheading harmless Louis XVI., the French had rid themselves of a mild "tyrant" or "despot"; they were soon to taste of the rule of a genuine tyrant, thus learning how mistaken all their former estimates of autocracy had been.

It was only a short time after the French government had thus been changed again in France, that the news arrived from America that George Washington had breathed his last. In making these tidings officially known, Bonaparte ordered the flags draped with crape for ten days, adding: "Washington is dead! That great man fought against tyranny. He established the liberty of his country. His memory will be ever dear to the freemen of both hemispheres, and especially to the French soldiers, who, like him and like the American troops, have fought for liberty and equality!"

Well would it have been for France had Bonaparte been actuated by the same unselfish motives as Washington! While he undoubtedly had the will, the power, and the capacity to direct everything, while he was a military genius and a great administrator, the lack of corresponding moral qualities prevented him from really becoming the greatest man the world has ever seen, although for a time he seemed to have attained that dizzy height.

The Consulate

Bonaparte's *coup d'etat* had, as we have seen, established a new form of government; but the new constitution was formally adopted only after having been submitted to the nation, each voter being asked to state whether he wished to see it adopted or not. By this plebiscite, or vote of the people, it was ascertained that more than 3,000,000 voters were in favor of its adoption, and only 1500 opposed, which proves how gladly it was welcomed by the nation in general. Indeed, as one man said, "The people are so weary, so disgusted with Revolutionary horrors and follies, that they are sure any change will be for the better."

The new Consulate was a republic with one man in reality supreme, that man being, of course, Bonaparte himself, the First Consul. Still, mainly to blind the people to this fact, a Senate and a Legislative Corps were chosen, though given little real power, and two other consuls (Cambaceres and Lebrun) were appointed, who, however, were so subordinate to the chief executive, or First Consul, that they were merely his advisers. Even at that time the most clear-sighted perceived that everything would henceforth center in Bonaparte, and one man remarked prophetically, "That young man has begun like Caesar, and I fear he will have the same end."

Bonaparte declared at the very outset, "In future, we will have no parties, no Jacobins, no Royalists, but only Frenchmen," and he showed his impartiality by appointing Talleyrand, a Royalist, and Fouche, a Jacobin, as ministers of Foreign Affairs and of the Police. His mottoes being, "Every career open to talent," and "The tools belong to him who can handle them," he picked out men regardless of their origin or station, considering only their fitness for the work he wished them to do. Before long (1802) he also instituted what is still a most popular and democratic order; that of the "Legion of Honor," whose members were to be recruited from those who had distinguished themselves in some way, thereby "deserving well from the country." With the perception of genius, the skill of a born administrator, and the untiring energy for which he was noted all through life, Bonaparte brought order out of chaos with marvelous rapidity, arranging things so that prosperity should return as fast as possible to a sorely stricken country.

In a very short time anarchy was ended, religion restored, exiles recalled, and trade recovering; for the country was so weary of the disorder and excesses of the last ten years that it was "ready to perform the impossible" to help him. The new and very capable hand at the helm soon steered the ship of state into much smoother waters, and, as confidence returned, even social life became gayer and more brilliant. The center of festivities now, as of old, was the Tui-

Empress Josephine

leries, for on the very day he was installed First Consul, Bonaparte decided to leave the Luxembourg,—where the Directors had sat,—and to take possession of the former abode of royalty. On perceiving the glaring "liberty caps and pikes" with which Revolutionary taste had decorated the palace, he said contemptuously, "Remove all those things; I don't like to see such rubbish!"—a remark which, a few years before, would doubtless have sent him to the guillotine.

While Bonaparte himself continued to be styled "Citizen First Consul," Josephine, who now did the honors of the palace most gracefully, was invariably called "Madame," and greeted by ambassadors and visitors of all kinds in the old courtly manner. She was a general favorite, and Bonaparte acknowledged how helpful her tact was when he once said, "I win battles, but Josephine wins hearts!"

You might think that Bonaparte could now feel satisfied with what he had accomplished. Evidently he was not, for when some one complimented him upon his achievements, he said: "Yes, I have done enough, it is true! In less than two years I have won Cairo, Paris, and Milan; but for all that, my dear fellow, were I to die to-morrow, I should not, at the end of ten centuries, occupy one half a page of general history!"

In beginning his new functions, Bonaparte declared that he was in favor of peace, and wrote fine letters to England and Austria to propose that the war be ended. But as he would conclude peace only in case they were willing to restore to France all that had recently been taken from her, his offers were not accepted,—a state of affairs which did not grieve him, for he remarked, "Conquest has made me what I am, and conquest alone can maintain me."

Therefore, about three months after assuming the title of First Consul, Bonaparte, having again pacified the Vendee, gave Moreau orders to continue his campaign against Austria from the north, and himself prepared to lead an army into Italy for the second time. But as the bulk of the Austrian forces were then busy besieging Genoa, the last stronghold of the French in Italy, and were thus close at hand to check any attempt to enter this country by the shore road, Bonaparte determined to lead his army over the Alps by the higher pass of St. Bernard, farther north. The enemy did not think it possible that Bonaparte would come that way; but Bonaparte often said that "impossible" is not a French word. The engineer sent by him to reconnoiter, objected to the great difficulties of this route, only to be interrupted by Bonaparte, who said, "Difficult, of course; the only question is, Can it be done?"

"Yes, provided we make extraordinary efforts!" replied the engineer.

Such an admission was all Bonaparte required, for he immediately said: "Enough. Let us depart at once."

While the army and supplies were being collected at Geneva, Bonaparte was completing his plans, and, just before leaving the Tuileries, showed his secretary a map of northern Italy, saying: "At this point, I shall cross the Po. Here I shall meet the enemy on the plains, and there," putting his finger near Marengo, "I shall fight and beat him!" This statement, as we shall see, time was to verify. Still, on leaving Paris, Bonaparte significantly remarked to his ministers, "Should anything happen, I shall be back like a thunderbolt!" for he did not intend to let any one attempt to overthrow *his* government or take his place at its head.

Having arrived at Geneva, Bonaparte visited Rousseau's grave, and was heard to wonder whether it would not have been better for France if that writer had never been, adding, "Well, the future must decide whether it would not have been better for the repose of the whole world if neither I nor Rousseau had ever lived!"

The foe were still wondering where Bonaparte was going to direct the army he was reviewing at Geneva, when the crossing of the St. Bernard—where there were no tunnels or even decent roads in those days—had already begun. In fact, roads were made as the army advanced, and cannon were taken to pieces, and either carried or dragged by the soldiers themselves. The barrels of heavy guns, set in hollow logs, were hauled by hundreds of soldiers up dizzy heights, so that in less than six days thirty-five thousand men, with all their artillery and baggage, had scaled the mountain, and were "rushing down from the Alps like a torrent!"

Bonaparte climbed the mountain also, mounted on one of the sure-footed donkeys of the region, led by an Alpine guide who little suspected the name or rank of his charge. To beguile this long climb over the St. Bernard, Bonaparte—who always tried to find out all he could about people—closely questioned this rustic guide, and finished by inquiring what was the man's greatest ambition. Thus learning that the man's highest hope was to purchase a small farm, properly stocked, Bonaparte greatly surprised him, soon after, by bestowing upon him the very place he had so well described!

Second Italian Campaign

By crossing the St. Bernard, Bonaparte's army arrived in Italy almost before the Austrian general, still at Genoa, could believe it was coming. All his plans were thus disconcerted, for he had intended to enter southern France as soon as Genoa was taken, to carry on the war there. Instead, he was now in danger of being captured. Hastening northward to escape, just as Bonaparte had foreseen, one Austrian force was defeated at Montebello; but the greatest battle of the war took place, a few days later, at Marengo (1800). Here the French, repulsed a first and a second time, were almost ready to yield, when Bonaparte cried: "One battle is lost, but there is still time to win another. My friends, we have had enough of this. You know it is my custom to sleep on the battlefield."

The soldiers, thrilled by his wonderful personal magnetism, and supported by the timely arrival of the troops under General Desaix, then won a glorious victory, the only thing which marred Bonaparte's exultation being the death of this officer, for he exclaimed, "Ah, what a fine day this would have been, could I have greeted Desaix on the battlefield to-night!"

By this victory, which forced this Austrian army to surrender, Bonaparte in a forty days' campaign recovered possession of the Cisalpine Republic he had founded; and four days later he had a solemn *Te Deum* sung in the Cathedral at Milan, thereby openly showing his intention thereafter to respect and uphold the Roman Catholic Church. The result of Bonaparte's successes in Italy and of Moreau's great victory at Hohenlinden, in Germany, was the treaty of Luneville with Austria (1801), whereby France was again extended to the

Rhine, and the Batavian, Helvetian, Ligurian, and Cisalpine republics were again confirmed.

Meantime, the army left in Egypt under Kleber had been sorely harassed by Turks and English, and the English had taken Malta. Then, Kleber having been murdered, his successor, despairing of maintaining his exposed position abroad, made an arrangement whereby he gave up Egypt, while the English, in exchange, undertook to convey his army back to France.

During their three years' occupation of Egypt, the French had effected many improvements, and their scientists had, besides, collected important data of all kinds. Among other things, the lost art of reading inscriptions on Egyptian monuments is due to this expedition. It seems that while the soldiers were digging a canal at Rosetta, they discovered a slab of stone on which was inscribed a certain decree written in three ways: in Greek, which could be easily read; in popular Egyptian, or demotic writing; and in the writing of Egyptian priests—hieroglyphics. As all three versions were almost uninjured,—being carved in very hard stone,—this inscription afforded the long-sought key for recovering the art of deciphering hieroglyphics. Still, this art was perfected only after long and patient study on the part of the French archaeologist Champollion and other noted scientists.

A year after the peace of Luneville with Austria, Bonaparte signed the famous treaty of Amiens with England, whereby the English pledged themselves to restore Malta to the Knights of St. John. But their failure to keep this promise, as we shall see, soon led to a renewal of the war, so this peace can be regarded as only an armistice.

Bonaparte, having ended warfare for the time being, triumphantly declared, "Now, I shall give myself to the administration of France!" That resolution was to bear very good fruits, for, as one writer says, "The genius of the First Consul was as marvelous in peace as in war, and he applied himself with unwearied labor to the promotion of internal prosperity in France. Day by day decrees were issued which repressed some abuse, conferred some benefit, commanded some useful public work; and soon the face of the land was renewed and society was quickened and refashioned by his touch. The émigrés were welcomed back if they chose to come;—public instruction was improved, though still separated from religion; the government of the provinces was organized anew; industry, commerce, agriculture, arts, and science began to flourish once more; and roads, fortresses, and harbors were repaired and strengthened."

Meanwhile a committee of learned men appointed by Bonaparte had long been working to provide a complete system of good and uniform laws for the whole country. He had directed them to select all that was good in former codes, making a new and practical one, in which each clause was to be short, simple, and clear. When the committee made its report, Bonaparte presided at the meetings of a council which revised the new code, and himself suggested many very wise changes. As a result, his great code of laws preserves most that was excellent in previous codes, although much modified by his love of brevity, and his practical views, for he used to say, "Every good must have common sense for its foundation." He was so justly proud of this piece of legal work, that he once declared, "I shall go down to posterity with the code in my hand!"

This code, which was issued in 1804, was called the *Code Civil*, or the *Code Napoleon*, and was adopted by many countries besides France. Although slightly changed, much of the Code, to all intents and purposes, is still in force in France, Belgium, Holland, Switzerland, Italy, Louisiana, and many Spanish-American countries.

Allegory of the Concordat of 1801 - Pierre Joseph Célestin François

It was in 1801 that arrangements were made to place the Church of France once more under the spiritual rule of the Pope. The treaty signed with him went by the name of the Concordat, and provided that the government should pay the salaries of the clergy. To celebrate its final signature a *Te Deum* was sung on Easter Day at Notre Dame, Bonaparte being present with all his staff. Thus, six years after the ancient cathedral had been desecrated by the worship of the Revolutionary goddess of Reason, Bonaparte restored Catholicism, saying, "In reviving a religion which has always prevailed in the country, in giving liberty of exercising their worship to the majority, I shall satisfy every one."

Murder of the Duke of Enghien

In the year 1802 Bonaparte who had first been elected consul for ten years had himself made consul for life, with the privilege of choosing his own successor. You must not imagine, however, that every one was perfectly satisfied to see Bonaparte at the head of affairs in France. There were—as there always are,—discontented people, who fancied *they* ought to occupy his place. Besides, the Royalists, who had hoped that as soon as order was restored, Louis XVIII. might be recalled to France (as Charles II. had been to England), were sorely disenchanted.

As their remonstrances had no effect, sundry conspiracies were formed during the Consulate to remove Bonaparte—the chief obstacle—out of their way. Once (in 1800) an infernal machine was set off in a narrow street, through which the consul was to pass on his way to the opera; but it went off just too late to injure him, although the explosion killed a large number of people. Three years later, a Vendee Royalist named Cadoudal headed a conspiracy, in which one of Napoleon's former friends, General Moreau, was slightly implicated. This general was exiled to America in punishment, while the leader and many others were beheaded.

Even before the treaty of Amiens, Bonaparte had established a camp at Boulogne as preparation for the old plan of invading England, which was then generally termed "perfidious Albion." Because the English did not give up Malta as they had promised, and because Bonaparte firmly demanded that they do so, it seemed as if these preparations might soon be useful.

Before one can make war successfully, however, money is a great consideration, and it was because he needed all the funds he could obtain to make war upon England, that the First Consul sold Louisiana to the United States government, for $15,000,000. Louisiana had belonged first to France, then to Spain, and had only recently been given back to her old allegiance; but Bonaparte feared that England might seize this colony, and, besides, as he stated when making the sale: "It is for the interest of France that America should be great and strong. I read farther ahead in the future than you do. I am preparing avengers of my wrongs."

Meantime, war had been going on in Haiti, which Toussaint L'Ouverture, "the Bonaparte of the Blacks," as he proudly styled himself, had proclaimed an independent republic. To recover possession of this rich colony, Bonaparte sent his brother-in-law thither with a strong army; but after various ups and downs the French were defeated, and the negroes made good their independence. Toussaint L'Ouverture, however, was made prisoner and conveyed to a dungeon in France, where—accustomed to a tropical climate—he died of cold and dampness after being imprisoned only a few months.

It was in 1803 that war with England began again. In answer to Bonaparte's demands that Malta be surrendered, the English seized 1200 French and Batavian ships. Bonaparte immediately retaliated by seizing as prisoners of war some 10,000 peaceful English subjects who were then sojourning in France.

In the following year, wishing "to strike terror in the hearts of the Bourbons even in London," and to put an end to the frequent conspiracies to restore them to the throne, Bonaparte ordered the arrest of the Duke of Enghien, the last of a younger branch of the Bourbon family (the Condés). This young prince was then in Germany, ten miles from the French frontier. Under the false pretext that he was involved in Cadoudal's conspiracy, Bonaparte ordered troops to cross the frontier, enter a neutral country, snatch the prince out of his bed, and bring him straight to a fortress near Paris. All was done exactly as the consul had ordered; then, on the very night of his arrival, the duke was summoned before a court-martial, tried without being given time to produce witnesses, and condemned to be shot like a spy, before daylight, in the castle moat!

Such a cruel deed of retaliation, which robbed a noble family of its last scion, and laid an indelible stain on Bonaparte's fame, was condemned by every one. Talleyrand remarked in his cynical way, "It is worse than a crime; it is a blunder!" Pitt, the great English statesman, said, "Bonaparte has now done himself more mischief than we have done him since the last declaration of war."

Still, crime as it was, the French in general did not resent it so deeply as other nations expected. On the contrary, and as if better to show their admiration for their hero and savior from anarchy, three days later they again offered Bonaparte the crown which he had already once, at least, refused. It was in May, at St. Cloud,—where the First Consul was wont to spend his summers,—that a deputation appeared, saying, "Citizen First Consul, you are founding a new era, but you must make it lasting; brilliancy is nothing without duration! When, in reply, Bonaparte invited them to make their whole thought known, the deputation replied, "The Senate thinks it is of the utmost interest to the French people to intrust the government of the Republic to Napoleon Bonaparte, Hereditary Emperor."

Although this invitation corresponded exactly with his secret wishes, Bonaparte made believe to hesitate, and it was only after the Senate's wish had been seconded by a majority of three million votes in its favor, that Bonaparte really became "Napoleon I., Emperor of the French." This title was suggested, both because the word "king" was still distasteful to Revolutionists, and also because "emperor," like "consul," was a reminder of glorious old Roman times.

The First Empire

The Empire having been proclaimed at St. Cloud on the 18th of May, 1804, Bonaparte adopted the usual royal and imperial custom, signing henceforth only his first name, Napoleon. He also proceeded to rearrange things to suit his new dignity, but postponed his coronation until December, so that it might be celebrated with more pomp and grandeur than had ever yet been displayed.

As "hereditary emperor," Napoleon felt that his relatives—who were always greedy for money and honors—should share in his good fortune. His mother, Letitia Bonaparte, henceforth known as Madam Mother (Madame Mere), and his brothers and sisters—who could now revel in the titles of princes and princesses—all received large annual incomes, which the younger people spent lavishly, while the mother, mindful of times when money had been scarce, hoarded for a possible needy future. Of this stern old lady Napoleon once said, "It is to my mother and to her good example that I owe everything;" but she disapproved of this new grandeur, and once when her son playfully held out his hand to her for a court salute, she exclaimed indignantly: "Not so, my son! It is your duty to kiss the hand of her who gave you life!"

All Napoleon's family gave him a great deal of trouble, as you will see, but it was only his mother and Lucien—the brother who once threatened to kill him if he attacked the liberties of the Republic—who thoroughly disapproved of his new title and elevation. Besides, an estrangement occurred because Napoleon tried to interfere in Lucien's marriage affairs; and as the mother sided with Lucien in all their quarrels, she was not present at the coronation, although Napoleon had her portrait inserted in the picture by the great court artist, David.

The companions in arms of Napoleon, sixteen in number, received the title of "Marshals of the Empire," their energetic master telling them: Succeed! I judge men by success!" Talleyrand, Napoleon's former fellow-consuls, and other leading civilians were also made prominent members of the newly organized imperial court, which was regulated according to many of the old rules of etiquette, modified, of course, to suit more advanced times.

While extensive preparations were being made for the grand coronation, Napoleon and Josephine set out on a journey, visiting the camp at Boulogne, where the new emperor was received by the mayor with the pompous speech, "God created Napoleon and then rested from his work!" Here, too, Napoleon reviewed "the Grand Army," sitting on Dagobert's throne and distributed Legion of Honor decorations, before proceeding to Cologne, inspecting improvements, forts, factories,—everything, in short,—on his way.

Anxious to imitate Charlemagne, his favorite hero, and to consecrate his elevation in the eyes of Catholic Europe, Napoleon induced the Pope to come to Paris for the coronation ceremony,—a favor granted solely because the restoration of Catholic religion in France was due mainly to him. Pope Pius VII., with his train of cardinals and priests, was welcomed at Fontainebleau by Napoleon in person, both host and guest little suspecting that they would a few years later assume the parts of jailer and prisoner in the selfsame palace.

On December 2, 1804, the court assembled in the Tuileries in gorgeous array, to await the appearance of Napoleon and Josephine. The emperor wore a long white satin robe embroidered with golden bees,—token of the old Frankish kings,—his royal-purple (red) velvet mantle, lined with ermine and weighing eighty pounds, being strewn with them also. His head was encircled by a wreath of golden laurel leaves like those worn by Roman emperors of old, and the new army standards were surmounted by golden eagles, which were to be the favorite emblem of the man so often compared to that soaring bird. Josephine, also in white satin, and with a royal mantle whose train was borne by her daughter and by Napoleon's sisters, was further adorned with an exquisite lace ruff, and with jewels of great price and magnificence.

In the midst of all this splendor, Napoleon suddenly caught a glimpse of a lawyer who had once tried to dissuade Josephine from marrying an impecunious officer by saying, "Madam, he has nothing but a soldier's sword and cape!" Napoleon now reminded him of that remark by pointing significantly to his jeweled sword and royal robes and saying proudly, Sir, behold the soldier's cape and sword!"

In a dazzling chariot of gold and plate glass,—bearing the imperial monogram "N," and drawn by eight white horses,— escorted by court and army in festive array, Napoleon and Josephine drove in state to Notre Dame. There, after the Pope had

Napoleon in his Coronation Robes - François Gérard

duly anointed him and consecrated his crown, Napoleon—who refused to *be* crowned by any one—placed the jeweled circle on his own head, and then crowned Josephine as she gracefully knelt before him.

Of course, all manner of festivities and rejoicings followed, but Napoleon and Josephine soon left Paris to hasten to Italy, where the Cisalpine Republic, having asked to become a kingdom, wished to bestow upon Napoleon the title of King of Italy. This second coronation took place in the beautiful cathedral of Milan, where Napoleon put on the old Lombard iron crown (a broad band of gold and jewels inclosing a narrow band of iron, said to be fashioned from one of the nails of the Crucifixion), repeating impressively the time-honored words, "God has given it to me; woe betide him; who touches it!"

Still, too many important matters were calling elsewhere for Napoleon to tarry long in Italy; so, after creating the Order of the Iron Crown, he gratified Josephine and pleased himself by naming his stepson, Eugene de Beauharnais, Viceroy of Italy. Next, having annexed Genoa and part of the Ligurian Republic to France, the emperor divided other parts of Italy into duchies, which became dependencies of the new French Empire.

The Battle of Austerlitz

That an "upstart" *(parvenu)* should dare assume the title of Emperor, and that a soldier should wear a royal crown, seemed so monstrous to aristocratic Europe, that England, Russia, Sweden, and Austria soon banded together in a coalition against France,—the third since royalty had been abolished. On hearing this news, Napoleon hastened back to Boulogne, hoping to be able to carry out at last the long-cherished plan of attacking England. But before England could be reached, the French had to cross the Channel with their armies. The troops assembled at Boulogne were so numerous that many vessels would be necessary to transport them, and such vessels, of course, needed to be escorted and protected by French men-of-war. Then, too, before the army could start, favorable winds were needed to swell the sails, for although Fulton had already experimented with a steamboat on the Seine, and he and Papin had offered their inventions to the French government, such means of propulsion were still considered wildly impractical. So also seemed the proposal to go in balloons, or to dig a tunnel under the sea so as to enable the soldiers to march across, although airships and submarine tunnels are now no longer novelties.

Meantime the English, alarmed by the preparations at Boulogne, made sundry brave attempts to enter that port and destroy the "nutshells" intended to convey hostile armaments to their shores. They also watched and pursued the French fleet of warships, which, hoping to give them the slip, dodged about the Atlantic, even sailing as far as the West Indies. The trick succeeded, but, on the return home, the French admiral made the mistake of stopping for repairs at Cadiz in Spain, where his fleet was soon bottled up by the wary foe. Knowing it useless to attempt to cross "that ditch"—as Napoleon contemptuously termed the English Channel—save under cover of a strong fleet, the French emperor wrathfully put off the invasion of England. Then, learning that the Austrians were attacking his ally, Bavaria, he determined to carry the war thither. In an incredibly short time, therefore, the Boulogne host marched eastward and at Ulm surrounded the Austrian general, who was forced to surrender with a large army! This was a grand triumph for the French soldiers, who, full of admiration for the general they adored, spoke jokingly of their long march, thus, "He has found another way of making war; he no longer makes us fight with our arms, but with our legs!"

On the very day after the surrender at Ulm, the French fleet was almost annihilated in the great naval battle of Trafalgar, where the English admiral Nelson lost his life, and the French admiral Villeneuve committed suicide rather than face Napoleon after such a disaster. The destruction of the French navy, of course, ended all chance of invading England; there was nothing, therefore, to prevent Napoleon's hurrying on to beat the armies of the Austrian and Russian emperors, before the Prussian king could make up his mind to join them.

As he passed some Austrian wounded, Napoleon's cordial salute, "Honor to the brave," showed that he could put himself in the enemy's place, although he was even then hurrying on "to conclude this campaign by a stroke of thunder!" His plan was to take Vienna,—where, the emperor having fled, resistance proved slight,—and to attack the allies, who stationed themselves on an advantageous height at Austerlitz. Napoleon, on learning this, determined to lure part of them from their position so as to take possession of it himself. His plans proved so successful that when morning broke,—on the first anniversary of his coronation (December 2, 1805),—all was favorably arranged for the "Battle of the Three Emperors," as it has also been called. Even the fog, which had hitherto veiled the foe's movements, was suddenly dispelled by the rays of the rising sun, which Napoleon hailed as "the sun of Austerlitz," an omen of good luck.

The soldiers, inspired by his triumphant assertion, "That army is mine!" and fired by one of his stirring speeches, filed rapidly past him, begging him with rough devotion to keep out of danger. As Napoleon had foreseen, the allies were routed, and as some of them fled over a frozen lake, his gunners pointed their cannon so that the heavy balls broke up the ice and the fugitives perished by drowning. By skillful maneuvering and brave fighting Napoleon beat his opponents so thoroughly that even one of the seasoned Austrian generals sadly declared he had "no conception of such a defeat!"

As for the French, they were jubilant, and the soldiers present never forgot Napoleon's laudatory speech: "Soldiers, I am proud of you. When you reenter your homes, you need but say. 'I was at Austerlitz!' and you will be welcomed with the cry, 'There is a hero!'" To his wife Napoleon wrote on this occasion: "I have beaten the Russian and Austrian armies, commanded by the two emperors. I am a little tired." But such was his marvelous endurance that a very few hours' sleep always sufficed to restore his strength.

This defeat at Austerlitz not only crippled the Austrian and Russian forces, but determined the Prussians, who were about to join them, to make friends with Napoleon instead. Hoping to obtain better terms of peace, the beaten Emperor of Austria now begged for an interview with Napoleon, who received him by a camp fire, saying playfully, "Here is the palace your Majesty compels me to occupy!" But after Austerlitz there was no further attempt on the part of this emperor to treat Napoleon otherwise than as an equal, and it was by the light of this bivouac that they settled the preliminaries for the peace of Pressburg, by which Austria gave up Tyrol and the Venetian territories. The Emperor of Austria soon after relinquished the title of "Emperor of the Holy Roman Empire" (really, Emperor of Germany)—which thus came to an end after existing a little more than a thousand years, 800–1806. He retained only the title "Hereditary Emperor of Austria," while many of the other German states formerly in the Empire now united to form the "Confederation of the Rhine," under the protection of France.

The Battle of Austerlitz - François Gérard

Seizing the excuse that while he was closely engaged in Austria, Naples had started to attack the French in Italy, Napoleon now declared, "The dynasty of Naples has ceased to reign," and sent an army to take possession of the kingdom of Naples, which he soon after bestowed upon his eldest brother, Joseph. Then, to his third brother, Louis,—who had married Josephine's daughter Hortense three years before,—Napoleon awarded the throne of Holland, and upon his sisters and marshals he conferred numerous duchies in Italy and Germany; for he knew the French would resent any new division of their soil, and disliked any addition to the ranks of their aristocracy.

On his way home from Pressburg, Napoleon stopped at Munich, where he announced the suppression of the old Republican Calendar, and witnessed the marriage of his stepson, Eugene, to a daughter of the King of Bavaria, his faithful ally in the recent war. On this occasion he formally promised that

Eugene should have the throne of Italy if he himself should die without a direct heir.

On returning to Paris, the emperor received a great ovation, the Senate bestowing upon him the title of "the Great." Then, too, the "Column of Austerlitz" (or of the "Grand Army") was fashioned from the cannon won in battle, the bronze spiral of bas-reliefs around it representing various episodes in the campaign. This column, crowned by a statue of Napoleon, was erected in the center of the Vendome Square, and is hence known also as the "Column Vendome." It still stands on the original spot, although its existence has been sorely endangered several times, and although, as we shall see, it was once actually thrown down by an angry mob!

Entry into Berlin

Napoleon's distribution of crowns and duchies proved another severe shock to conservative European monarchs, who argued that "if a king of royal lineage like Ferdinand of Naples can be summarily deposed, and a commoner like Joseph Bonaparte placed on the throne in his stead, no kingdom in Europe will henceforth be secure!" To prevent a similar fate from overtaking them, they felt that all sovereigns should band together against this bold innovator and chastise him for his presumption.

This was the general verdict, and it gave rise to the Fourth Coalition (1806), to which England contributed funds, while Prussia and Russia did the main part of the fighting. Napoleon, who had been watching proceedings closely, and had made ready for war by collecting forces and supplies in the states of his German allies, now deemed it best that operations should begin before the allies could make further preparations. With that purpose in view, he had his court journal publish such offensive articles about the Prussians in general, and about their beautiful Queen Louise in particular, that every loyal Prussian rose up in wrath against him. Even before war was openly declared, Napoleon was on his way to attack the Prussians, exciting his ignorant soldiers the while by insisting that the foe was "insulting the victors of Austerlitz!"

By masterly tactics, Napoleon managed to place himself in the rear of two Prussian armies, and to attack one of them with overwhelming forces at Jena where the queen herself had been reviewing and encouraging the Prussian troops. Here Napoleon, torch in hand, himself superintended the placing of his guns, and quickly won another of his great victories. The picture of Napoleon at Jena, by Vernet, shows the emperor at the moment when, reviewing his troops, he overhears an impatient soldier whispering urgently, "Forward, forward!" To these words the great general severely replies: "What's this? It can be only a beardless youth who tries to prescribe what I shall do. Let him wait until he has commanded in twenty pitched battles, before pretending to give me any advice!"

On the same day one of Napoleon's generals defeated the other Prussian army (at Auerstadt, a few miles north of Jena), so Prussia's strength was annihilated for a time. In spite of the heroic courage and dauntless patriotism of the people the French soon gained possession of the large fortress of Magdeburg, and at the end of a three weeks' campaign entered Berlin as conquerors.

This triumphal entrance of the French army into Berlin, and the ungenerous conduct of the emperor toward people and queen, rankled sorely in Prussia for many a year, as did the fact that he bore off to Paris, as a trophy, the sword which lay on Frederick the Great's coffin, and which had once gloriously carved the fortunes of the country. Besides, Napoleon made the vanquished pay for the war, vindictively saying in regard to the Prussian nobles, "I will make them so poor that they shall be obliged to beg their bread!" This, as you perceive, was not chivalrous, but Napoleon was truthful and generous only when it suited his ends to appear so, and proudly considered himself the rest of the time above observing the usual laws of conduct and morality. Still, he rewarded the Germans who helped him, by making the Saxon duke a king, and by organizing properly the Confederation of the Rhine.

It was while in Berlin that Napoleon devised a plan to ruin England without invading that country. This consisted in forbidding any of the continental European countries to allow her ships in their ports, to buy any of her goods, or to sell her any supplies. As England is largely a manufacturing country, and depends upon selling her manufactured products abroad,—getting raw materials and food in exchange,—this blockade, if strictly carried out, meant little less than ruin and starvation for her. To help in making the blockade strict, Napoleon decreed that all Englishmen found in continental countries should be made prisoners of war, and that no letter written in English or addressed to any Englishman should be allowed to pass into or out of the continent. Such was the fear Napoleon inspired that nearly all the European nations in time submitted, or pretended to submit, to this "Continental System," or "Continental Blockade." As a result, England was somewhat crippled, and the continental countries also were injured by the interference with trade that had been profitable to both parties; but so many English goods were smuggled in that the blockade proved a failure.

It was also at Berlin that Napoleon performed an act of spectacular generosity in favor of the German governor of the city, Von Hatzfeld, who had been left there in command on condition that he should be loyal to Napoleon, rather than to his own country. But a letter written by Von Hatzfeld to the Prussians, betraying some of Napoleon's plans, accidentally fell into the French emperor's hands. The governor's wife, deeming her husband innocent, yet knowing that he would be shot if court-martialed, fell at Napoleon's feet, wildly beseeching his intervention, until he showed her the letter proving her husband's guilt. Seeing the poor woman almost swoon at this revelation, Napoleon suddenly gave the letter to her, bidding her cast it into the fire with her own hand, thus destroying the only proof of her husband's treachery. You can imagine with what joy the wife obeyed, and how grateful she felt thereafter to the man to whom her husband owed his life!

Death of Queen Louise

When the Prussians were conquered, Napoleon set out to attack his other enemies, the Russians, although winter had already set in, and his army had to march through snow and slush across Poland, suffering untold hardships before it could reach Warsaw. Some twelve years before this, the ancient kingdom of Poland had been conquered and its territory divided among Russia, Austria, and Prussia. Now, the French were everywhere warmly welcomed by the Poles, who, hoping Napoleon would restore their national independence, joined him in hosts, and helped him win the desperate battle of Eylau (1807), when he was attacked by Russian forces twice as large as his own.

While Napoleon was still in winter camp in Poland, Alexander I., the Russian emperor, collected new forces, which Napoleon routed the next summer in the battle of Friedland (1807). Then, believing it unwise to continue the struggle any longer, Alexander sued for peace, and agreed to meet Napoleon on a raft in the river Niemen, near Tilsit, to discuss terms. The two armies, drawn up on either bank, saw the emperors meet and embrace. We are informed that Alexander opened the conversation on this historic occasion by exclaiming, "I hate the English as much as you do!"

"In that case peace is assured," replied Napoleon, whose main object at present was to induce Russia to join in the Continental Blockade.

In the interview on the raft, Alexander not only gave up a part of his share of Poland, but faithfully promised "to close his door to the English," as well as to pay part of the costs of the war, while Napoleon won his opponent's heart by proposing to divide the world with him, leaving him to win lands from Sweden and Turkey.

While Alexander and Napoleon were thus conversing, the King of Prussia was uneasily riding up and down on the bank, conscious that his ally and his foe were settling his fate. Such was indeed the case, for in the treaty of Tilsit (1807) it was decided that the Prussian lands west of the Elbe should henceforth form the new kingdom of Westphalia for Napoleon's brother Jerome, while the duchy of Warsaw, which was to be governed by the King of Saxony, should be carved principally from Prussia's share of Poland. Thus, you see, the Poles' hopes were only partly fulfilled, for instead of restoring the kingdom of Poland and giving back all the lands seized by its three powerful neighbors, Napoleon allowed Austria—with which he was then on friendly terms—to retain all her share, and took only Prussia's and a part of Russia's.

Having thus settled matters with Russia, Napoleon next met the King and Queen of Prussia at Tilsit, the latter having come thither in hopes of helping her husband secure better terms. But, whereas her grace and beauty might have won concessions from Napoleon before his mind was fully made up, he always proved unchangeable, once a decision had been made. We are told that in the course of this momentous interview, Napoleon offered the lovely young queen a rose, which she took, asking archly (with reference to the fortress which Prussia was especially anxious to recover), "With Magdeburg, Sire?" But he sternly replied, "Madam, it is mine to give, yours to accept what I offer!" This ungallant answer proved the "last straw," for the delicate young queen was already so worn out with anxiety for her husband and country, and was grieving so sorely over the sufferings of her people, that she passed away (1810), saying (like Mary of England in regard to Calais), "Were they to open my heart, they would find 'Magdeburg' engraved upon it!"

This Louise of Prussia left two sons, one of whom was to be made the first Emperor of United Germany, after cruelly avenging her wrongs upon the French, as you will see.

Jerome's Marriages

Once more Napoleon returned to Paris, so full of his own importance, and so sure of himself, that he now became indeed more despotic than any Bourbon had ever dared to be. His wishes were supreme in every branch of the government, and while he retained a Senate and a Legislative Corps, they seemed to exist only to vote him soldiers and money as he demanded them. But everything seemed so prosperous and serene that France deemed her future fully assured.

Such was Napoleon's excessive vanity at this epoch that no one dared address him save in words of fulsome praise and adulation. This arrogance became simply unendurable to Talleyrand, who, although a Royalist, had hitherto served the Empire with ability and zeal. It is true that he had been rewarded by wealth and titles, but when he ventured to show that he thought a government unsafe which depended only on success for its existence, he grievously incurred Napoleon's displeasure. In fact, the emperor became so unbearably rude to his minister, that the latter revenged himself by saying, "What a pity it is that so great a prince should be so ill-bred!" and in 1809 actually left his service.

It was on his return from the glorious campaign of 1807 that Napoleon planned the erection of a "Temple of Glory"—now the Church of the Madeleine—besides erecting a triumphal arch in the great court between the palaces of the Louvre and Tuileries (Arche du Carrousel) and planning another, the Triumphal Arch of the Star, at the end of the beautiful drive of the Champs Elysees, or Elysian Fields. From this arch, Napoleon planned long avenues to radiate like the rays from a star, the principal one bearing the name of "the Grand Army," and the others those of his devoted marshals. It is, however, a disputed matter whether this triumphal arch derives its name from Napoleon's pet superstition concerning "his star," from this plan in regard to the avenues, or from the Order of the Star in the Legion of Honor, which the emperor founded.

Very soon after his return from Tilsit, Napoleon ordered the marriage of his youngest brother Jerome—then twenty-two—with the beautiful princess of Wurttemberg. Now, you must know that Jerome Bonaparte had journeyed, as a youth, to the United States, where he had married, at eighteen, a Miss Patterson of Baltimore. When this marriage took place, Jerome was, of course, under age, and such a union in France, without the consent of parents or guardians, is considered illegal. Jerome's family were furious about it, and Napoleon, after becoming emperor, became anxious to break this tie so that his brothers by espousing a princess, might win a royal alliance for the family. At first, boy as he was, Jerome refused to give up his young wife, but Napoleon artfully contrived to separate him from the lady, and then threatened or bribed him into compliance with his arbitrary wishes.

The Arc de Triomphe, depicted in a 1920s postcard

At Napoleon's order, therefore, the Senate declared Jerome's American marriage null, and offered the lady a sum of money to renounce all further right to the name of Bonaparte. Although she nobly refused, and rightly persisted in considering herself Jerome's lawful wife, the French emperor never

99

paid any heed to her or her children's claims, but concluded the royal marriage just as was planned. Then, after a ceremonious presentation at the imperial court, Jerome and his new wife proceeded to Westphalia, where they began their joint reign with much splendor.

As Napoleon's will was now supreme, he next proceeded to dispose of things in Italy, and joined Tuscany to France. Then, becoming incensed against the Pope for not observing the Continental Blockade, he suddenly revoked the gift which Charlemagne had made to the Holy See. For this and other reasons the Pope promptly excommunicated Napoleon, who, in return, had the Pope arrested, confined at various places, and finally brought captive to Fontainebleau, where he was to remain until 1814.

Meantime, so many countries had joined the Continental Blockade, that England had no important open market in Europe save in Portugal. As it proved easy to smuggle goods thence to all parts of the continent, Napoleon sternly bade Portugal join the blockade, also. When he heard that this imperial and imperious mandate was not immediately obeyed, Napoleon declared, "The House of Braganza has ceased to exist," and sent Junot at the head of an army to Portugal with orders to take possession of the country. The Portuguese royal family, not strong enough to resist such a foe, fled from Lisbon to Brazil, where the House of Braganza continued "to exist" and rule; but, after their hasty flight, Portugal itself fell an easy prey to the French.

Next, under the pretext of settling a quarrel in the Spanish royal family, and of quelling riots caused thereby, French armies entered Spain, and Napoleon induced King Charles IV. and the crown prince Ferdinand to meet him at Bayonne, where he either tricked or bribed them both to cede the crown of Spain to his brother Joseph. Having already been appointed King of Naples, Joseph was now ordered to give that kingdom to Murat,—Napoleon's friend and the husband of his sister Caroline,—so as to mount the throne of Spain. But it is one thing to become king, and quite another to remain so. The proud Spaniards, not liking to have a monarch forced upon them, soon rebelled, and drove Joseph out of Madrid. Thereupon, Napoleon promptly sent troops to restore him and reduce the Spaniards to obedience. But the English just as promptly sent troops to aid the Spaniards, having previously helped Portugal to drive away her French rulers. The resulting war, waged by the Spanish, Portuguese, and English against the French, is known as the Iberian or Peninsular Campaign, and lasted from 1808 to 1814. This fighting proved excellent training for officers and soldiers, and enabled them to win great victories later on.

Napoleon, who had meantime gone to an important conference at Erfurt, where he renewed his vows of friendship with Alexander, dazzled every one there with his magnificence. To entertain his guests, the great French tragedian Talma was brought from Paris to play before "a pitful of kings," and it was here, too, that Napoleon had a memorable interview with Goethe and Wieland, the greatest German writers of the time.

Josephine Divorced

The gayeties of Erfurt once over, Napoleon proceeded to Spain, and began his campaign by a few victories which replaced Joseph on the throne at Madrid. But before the conquest of Spain could be completed, he received such alarming news from home that he hastily departed, leaving behind him some of his best generals and troops, with instructions to "drive the English into the sea." The French in Spain had to contend with English armies under Sir John Moore and Wellesley (later Duke of Wellington) in a number of pitched battles, and to wrest from the Spaniards themselves several towns by costly sieges; they were, besides, constantly worried by a species of guerrilla warfare, which the mountainous nature of the country made easy for the natives. The constant drain of men and money demanded by this war, proved, in time, Napoleon's ruin, he himself saying, later on, "It divided my strength, opened a way for the English, and injured my reputation throughout Europe." But he saw all this too late, although Talleyrand had predicted that it would prove "the beginning of the end."

Having left Spain,—never to return there,—Napoleon posted northwards; but whereas he generally traveled rapidly in a coach ingeniously fitted out so he could work even while journeying, on this occasion he rode horseback, eighty-five miles in five hours, using, of course, a number of horses, which he changed at various points on the route, for his only fast gait was a mad gallop. Napoleon's haste was due to the fact that Austria, deeming him safely occupied elsewhere, had suddenly thought this a fine opportunity to take her revenge. She was encouraged in this view by England,—Napoleon's inveterate foe—so a Fifth Coalition had been planned; but when she now invaded Bavaria, it was only to be confronted and beaten, to her intense surprise and dismay, in five battles on five successive days, by Napoleon and his allies of the Confederation of the Rhine. At Ratisbon, on the fifth day, Napoleon was wounded in the foot by a spent ball. The news of this injury caused such excitement and despair among the men that the emperor hardly waited until the bandage was fastened, before he remounted and reappeared among the troops, by whom he was madly cheered.

The road now being clear, Napoleon marched on to Vienna, which he entered for the second time in triumph. Then, on the way to attack the main Austrian army, the French troops distinguished themselves greatly at the crossing of the Danube, where bridges had to be built under great difficulties, and where was fought a bloody battle (Aspern). Finally came another famous victory at Wagram, after which Napoleon took up his abode at Schonbrunn, where he barely escaped the dagger of an assassin, and where he little suspected his son would spend his last days more than a score of years later.

Meanwhile, the Tyrol, which Napoleon had wrested from Austria and bestowed upon Bavaria, was in revolt against her new rulers. Under Andreas Hofer and a few other brave peasant leaders, these mountaineers expelled the Bavarians and heroically defended their beloved country step by step. Army after army sent against them met defeat, but in the end the Tyrolians were overcome. Hofer himself was taken and slain (1810) with some thirty other patriots, whose fame will endure forever in that picturesque region.

The war between Austria and France was ended by the peace of Vienna (1809), confirming previous treaties, but giving the Illyrian Provinces (Istria, Dalmatia, etc.) to France, and some smaller territories to Napoleon's allies. Such was the fame Napoleon won by these repeated triumphs, that we are told "he looked like one walking in a halo of glory," and he became such a popular idol, that

France gave herself to him, absorbed herself in him, and seemed at one time no longer to think save through him!"

Napoleon, like his admirers, now began to believe that he was the only man who could make and keep France great and prosperous, and the thought that the time would surely come when he would die, filled his own and many other hearts with nameless fears. As he and Josephine had no children, the Senate had conferred upon Napoleon, with the title of emperor, the right to adopt a successor; if Napoleon had no son, and adopted none, the throne was to go to certain of his brothers and their sons.

The Divorce of the Empress Josephine – Henri Schopin

The succession was a delicate matter, for while Napoleon would have liked to name his stepson, Eugene de Beauharnais, he knew perfectly well that his family would never countenance such a choice. For a brief time, therefore, Napoleon thought of adopting and training a nephew,—the son of his brother

Louis and stepdaughter Hortense,—but this child died young, and the emperor's affections never seemed to center upon any of his other nephews in the same way. Meantime, many people did not scruple to suggest that he divorce Josephine and marry again to secure an heir—a suggestion which Napoleon repudiated indignantly at first, but decided to adopt shortly after signing the treaty of Vienna.

When told at Fontainebleau what sacrifice she was expected to make for the sake of France, poor Josephine swooned from grief; but she was so brave and unselfish that, in spite of the fact that her heart was breaking, she finally consented to all Napoleon asked. Knowing that the captive Pope would never grant the desired divorce, the Senate and an ecclesiastical council were asked to pronounce it; and, in the presence of Napoleon, of her two children, and of a few of the great dignitaries, Josephine signed the paper by which she consented to this separation from the man she loved.

Then, still escorted by her devoted children, Josephine withdrew to Malmaison,—a country house she had bought while Napoleon was in Egypt,—where, honored and admired as much as ever, still bearing the title of empress, and provided with a fine pension, she quietly spent her few remaining years. Napoleon called there to see her sometimes, but such interviews proved too painful for both to be frequent at first, and, after his second marriage, roused such jealous feelings in the breast of the new empress that they had to be discontinued. Until his divorce, Napoleon had been wonderfully successful, and because his luck turned shortly after his second marriage, and because the repudiation of Josephine was not viewed with favor by the people in general, it was later said, "When Napoleon divorced himself from Josephine, he seemed to have divorced himself from his good genius."

Napoleon's Second Marriage

After Josephine had left the Tuileries forever, Napoleon found the palace so lonely that he removed to the Trianon, where nothing reminded him of his divorced wife. Then the question arose, Whom should he marry? For a man in his position, a princess seemed the only suitable wife, and he first suggested a marriage with the sister of his friend Alexander, who asked for time to consider. Then the impatient Napoleon asked for the eldest daughter of the Austrian emperor, Maria Louisa, or Marie Louise, a girl of eighteen. The Austrian emperor and his minister Metternich, afraid to offend their former foe, and anxious, besides, to secure lasting peace by this alliance, soon consented, so a marriage by proxy was celebrated in Vienna, before the new empress set out for France to join the husband she had never seen.

Their first meeting was arranged to take place at the French castle where Louis XVI. and Marie Antoinette had first met; but Napoleon rode on to meet the carriage, which he unexpectedly entered at the last relay. Thus the imperial couple arrived together at the castle, whence they went on to St. Cloud the next day, and then, in the gilded coronation carriage, to Paris. We are told that they paused to hear speeches under a temporary arch at the head of the Champs Elysees, before driving on to the Tuileries for a state marriage ceremony in the Square Hall in the Louvre. Here great pomp was displayed, the emperor's sisters and Hortense bearing Marie Louise's train; but the festive occasion was marred by Napoleon's wrath when he discovered that certain of the cardinals—who considered his divorce from Josephine invalid—were not present, as he had commanded. In his anger, the emperor banished these cardinals from court, and forbade them to wear their red robes in public until they had apologized; that is why these prelates, who upheld their principles with great dignity, are known in history as "the Black Cardinals."

Napoleon was more than double the age of the new empress, who was neither so graceful nor so gracious as her predecessor. To be sure, Marie Louise was only a girl at that time, but she never developed into so clever and charming a woman as Josephine, who had helped Napoleon in every way to reach his present position and success, while the new wife was, on the contrary, to hamper him before long. Still, at first, all proved rose-colored, and fetes were given everywhere to the imperial couple, who met nothing but cheers and adulation as they journeyed from place to place.

This marriage took place in 1810. During the same year, finding his brother Louis too devoted to the good of the Dutch to force them to ruin themselves by respecting the Continental Blockade, Napoleon arbitrarily removed him from the throne, and united Holland to France, saying playfully that it belonged by right to that country, for it was formed of "the sediment of French rivers!"

That year, also, the Swedes persuaded their childless king to adopt Bernadotte, one of Napoleon's old lieutenants, who, like Louis, quickly became too loyal to his adopted country to sacrifice its welfare to the emperor's ambitions. The dynasty founded by Bernadotte still reigns in Sweden.

During this brief time of comparative peace,—war was still going on in Spain,—Napoleon was busy planning many new improvements, and visiting many factories, for he made it a point to encourage talent wherever he found it. To supply work for the various great artists of his day (David, Gros, Gerard, Guerin, Prudhon), the vain emperor had them picture his battles, coronation, and marriage; he and the two empresses sitting for the many portraits which now adorn the French picture galleries. Engineers, architects, and scientists, also, had all the work they could do; and literature was duly encouraged, although the two greatest French writers of the day, Chateaubriand and Madame de Stael, foes of the emperor, were living in exile, and thus some of their greatest works were written out of the country. That Napoleon regretted the dearth of great literary lights at his court, is proved by his saying, "Had Corneille lived in my day, I should have made a prince of him!" You see, Napoleon was so fond of tragedy,—then admirably played by Talma,—that nothing would have pleased him better than to have his reign marked by literary masterpieces as was that of Louis XIV.

Napoleon's child—so longed for—was born on the 10th of March, 1811. Everybody, of course, hoped for a boy to inherit the imperial crown, and it had been arranged to announce a birth in the Tuileries by firing twenty-one guns for a daughter and one hundred for a son. You can imagine, therefore, how breathlessly people counted the shots, and with what cheers they greeted the booming of the twenty-second gun! Then Napoleon himself appeared at a window, holding his newborn treasure for all to see, while the semaphores (signal telegraphs) spread the happy tidings, which were everywhere received with great rejoicings, no one being more glad, or congratulating Napoleon more cordially, than poor deserted Josephine.

The possession of this son, who received at birth the title of "King of Rome," seemed to fill Napoleon's cup of bliss and prosperity; feeling the future assured, he now began to plan far ahead, his care for the administration by of the empire proving, if anything, greater than ever. And it was a very large section of Europe that Napoleon thus governed, for France had annexed Belgium, Holland, and a large part of Italy, besides Germany as far as the Rhine, while many kingdoms and duchies elsewhere were also subject to her emperor.

Napoleon was the kind of man who had blindly enthusiastic friends, as well as bitter enemies; he was, besides, generally surrounded by flatterers, who fostered his vanity by making such remarks as this: "Sire, some say that you are a god, others that you are a devil, but all unite in agreeing that you are more than a man!" Can you wonder that after a few years of such adulation his head was somewhat turned, and that he learned to believe himself infallible? But Napoleon was to exemplify to the utmost the old saying that "pride goes before a fall."

The Russian Campaign

We have seen how Napoleon and Alexander had sworn friendship on the raft in the Niemen and at Erfurt, and how they planned to divide Europe between them. But after the birth of an heir, Napoleon began to think that two masters in Europe might quarrel, especially as Alexander was no longer so friendly. You see, the Russian emperor had by this time discovered that Napoleon's promises could not be relied upon, and when Napoleon—whose rudeness passed all bounds at times—called him to order like a naughty schoolboy for not enforcing with sufficient severity the Continental Blockade, their relations became so strained that they were soon open foes.

In 1812, therefore, England, Russia, and Spain began the Sixth Coalition, which all the other European nations were in time to join, and which was to pursue its work until Napoleon had twice fallen from the dizzy heights to which genius and ambition had raised him. Napoleon's downfall was due, 1st, to his measureless ambition, which threatened to annihilate every other power; 2nd, to the fact that he would listen to neither argument nor advice, but deemed himself infallible; 3rd, to his obstinate attempts to enforce the Continental Blockade, thus angering many Europeans, while injuring England little; 4th, to his rash and obstinate war in Spain, by which he tied up an important part of his army; 5th, to his attack on Russia, where, instead of fighting against men only, he also had to face a deadly climate.

Napoleon began the fatal Russian campaign contrary to the advice or wishes of his ablest marshals, whose arguments he silenced with his old refrain, "The French love glory; to give them glory is to give them happiness!" But the emperor forgot that campaigns can end in defeat as well as in glory. Alexander proved wiser, and clearly perceiving that some of Napoleon's German allies were loyal only because they feared him, said, "If the Emperor Napoleon should experience a reverse, the whole of Germany would rise up to oppose his retreat or to prevent the arrival of his re-enforcements!"

Just before starting, Napoleon held a brilliant reunion of all the royalties and aristocracy at Dresden, where for the last time all paid homage to him, no one suspecting how soon all his magnificence would come to an end. After the festivities were over, court attire was laid aside, and the emperor, having bidden his wife farewell, set out to invade Russia with nearly half a million men of different nationalities, for every subordinate country had been asked to send troops for his use.

It was with a large part of this mixed "army of twenty nations" that Napoleon himself crossed the Niemen and pursued a Russian army into the heart of the country. The Russians, however, were fleeing before him merely so as to lure him on, and were destroying everything as they passed, so that the invaders had to bring their supplies over longer and longer distances. Nevertheless, knowing that great stores had been collected at Moscow,—where he intended to quarter his forces in comfort for the winter season,—Napoleon hastened boldly on.

Twice on the way, the Russians turned and fought bloody battles, and were defeated but not destroyed, first at Smolensk and then at Borodino (1812). Here, on the eve of the struggle, the emperor received a portrait of the baby King of Rome, which he proudly set up outside his tent, so that officers and men could admire it. Then, saying his child was still too young and innocent to gaze upon such sights as awaited them on the morrow, he ordered this picture carefully packed up.

When Moscow—the sacred city and then the capital of Russia—was reached, Napoleon was surprised to find it deserted and to be allowed to enter without opposition. Fearing some ambush, the French marched in warily, surprised to find only a few stragglers in the streets, instead of the usual 300,000 inhabitants. Even prisons were empty, the Russian general having liberated all captives before leaving; but, although the Russians had apparently abandoned everything to the foe, some of them had, in reality, made very clever preparations to frustrate all Napoleon's carefully made plans.

The Retreat!

On the day after the invading army marched into Moscow, while they were planning to settle there in winter quarters to recruit their strength, fire suddenly broke out in several parts of the city at the same time. At first this conflagration was thought to be accidental, but when no fire apparatus could be discovered (the Russians had destroyed or removed everything of the kind), and when the flames began to spread with lightning-like rapidity, Napoleon suddenly realized that this was the work of the enemy, who to foil him had sacrificed their Holy City!

Fed by trains of powder and hidden stores of inflammable materials, the fire raged madly, the furious and changing gales of the autumn helping it on, until nearly the whole city was a seething furnace. At the end of three awful days and nights, nine tenths of the houses there were in ashes.

Napoleon Surveys a Burning Moscow

With difficulty, Napoleon and his men escaped from the burning capital, and after some further delay in hopes of reaching an understanding with the Russian emperor, or Czar, they set out to return home. But the early Russian winter had already set in, so the retreat was conducted much of the way in the midst of driving snow, by troops unaccustomed to a severe climate, and neither clothed nor otherwise equipped to bear cold properly. Besides, all supplies were so scanty, that even the starving horses had to be killed for food! For eight weeks, therefore, the army trudged wearily on, discipline and order being soon forgotten by most of them, each man trying only to get over the frozen plain as best he could. The men were, besides, continually harassed by the pursuing Russians, and had to keep up a continuous running fight. Forced to bivouac at night by insufficient fires, with no other covering than the snow, thousands simply froze to death in their sleep, their stripped bodies being left by their companions a prey to the wolves.

As supplies along the route had been destroyed, and as the horses died of starvation, even the emperor trudged many weary miles on foot, living on the scantiest fare, yet encouraging his men by sharing all their hardships. It would be impossible to tell you of the despair caused by the cold, the deep snow, the sudden thaw and thick mud, then the colder and colder weather; the long road strewn with corpses and abandoned munitions of war; and the constant terror caused by bands of Cossacks attacking the sides and rear, slaying or capturing all those who tarried or straggled off in search of provisions. But during those eight weeks, countless deeds of heroism were performed, and Marshal Ney, who had charge of the rear guard, covered the retreat, step by step, actually using a musket like any of his men, and thus earning his proudest title, that of Bravest of the Brave."

Several times the host was in great danger, and once the emperor in person had to charge at the head of his guard. But the climax of this tragic retreat was reached on the banks of the Beresina River, where the ice proved too thin to serve as a bridge. Those who ventured on it were lost, and the bridge builders, standing for hours in the icy waters, perished in scores. Scarcely were the bridges ready when people began to hurry across, crowding so that even the emperor owed his safety only to his coachman's skill and daring. Part of the army got across in safety, but then came the mob of fugitives, crushing each other ruthlessly in their mad haste. Finally, when Russian grapeshot began to pour down upon this spot, the bridges, unable to support the stampeding multitude, suddenly collapsed, hurling their human freight into the icy waters. It is said that the Russians afterwards picked up and burned no less than twenty-four thousand dead bodies on the banks of this fatal stream.

Early in December, the emperor learned that in the absence of tidings from the snowbound army, a rumor of his death had arisen, and that a conspiracy had been formed, which had nearly overthrown his carefully established government! Feeling that he must reach Paris, and hold the reins of government in his own firm hand when the news of the Russian disaster became known there, Napoleon left Murat, Ney, and his other generals to direct the remainder of the retreat as best they could, and, by posting on night and day, reached his capital before any one even suspected he was coming. But it was only little by little that he allowed the full extent of the loss of life caused by the Russian campaign to become known, for out of the half million men who started, less than 100,000—some say only 20,000—ever returned. And of the 150,000 Frenchmen in that proud host which had set out only a few months before, there were left only a handful of tattered, emaciated, crippled survivors.

The story of the awful suffering during the retreat sorely wrung the hearts of mothers, widows, and orphans, kindling deep indignation against a sovereign who could expose his subjects to such suffering solely to satisfy his tremendous ambition. Even the soldiers, not comprehending the claims of politics, resented Napoleon's desertion of them, saying: What! is it thus that he abandons those of whom he calls himself the father? Where, then, is the genius who in the height of prosperity exhorted us to bear our sufferings patiently? He who lavished our blood, is he afraid to die with us? Will he treat us like the army of Egypt, to whom he became indifferent when by a shameful flight he found himself free from danger?" That desertion, which so rankled in the hearts of the soldiers, proved, besides, a bad example, for several officers also forsook their troops, leaving Ney and a few kindred spirits to bear the full brunt of the sufferings caused by the retreat. But Ney proved a real hero, for he stood by his men to the very end, throwing away his gun only after discharging it a last time at the pursuing foe, and plunging last of all into the icy Niemen, across which he swam to safety.

The Campaign of 1813

Just as soon as the disaster in Russia became fully known, Alexander's prediction was partly justified, for some of the German states abandoned Napoleon to join the Sixth Coalition, and turned upon him to avenge their losses. Prussia, which he had so humiliated, made truly heroic sacrifices to arm against him, the women selling even their fine hair and wedding rings to increase the war fund. Thus, in 1813, Napoleon found himself seriously threatened; but, still faithful to his old tactics, he determined to strike the first blow instead of waiting to be attacked. With French regiments composed of mere boys,—for he had been obliged to antedate the usual conscriptions,—and with the troops supplied by such German states as still remained loyal to him, he defeated the Russians and Prussians in the hard-fought battles of Lutzen and Bautzen. These successes, however, he so greatly exaggerated to reassure the French, that people began to use the expression "as false as the bulletin," as a mild substitute for the word "lie." Moreover, these triumphs in Germany were more than offset by severe losses in Spain, whence the French were driven by Wellington, who threatened even to invade southern France.

Deeming the opportunity favorable, the Emperor of Austria sent his prime minister Metternich to Dresden, to persuade Napoleon to make peace. But the conditions offered were so humiliating to the French emperor's pride, that he indignantly refused them, and when Metternich gravely reminded him that a continuation of the war would probably cost the lives of some 200,000 men, he made the brutal reply, "What do I care for 200,000 lives?" His worst offense, however, consisted in asking Metternich ironically how much the English were paying him to talk thus. This insult Metternich never forgot, and he duly avenged it, although keen enough to realize that there was, after all, considerable truth in the statement Napoleon then made: "Your sovereigns, born on the throne, may be beaten twenty times and reenter their capitals. I cannot, because I am a soldier who has risen from the ranks. My domination will not survive the day when I shall cease to be strong, and consequently feared."

It was after this momentous interview, and only because Napoleon obstinately refused to make peace, that his father-in-law joined the Coalition. Among its other supporters, by this time, were Bernadotte, Napoleon's old lieutenant, and Moreau, who had conspired against the First Consul and had since been an exile.

While the allied armies were constantly growing larger, Napoleon still won the battle of Dresden, where Moreau was slain; but he was at last badly defeated in the three days' "Battle of the Nations," at Leipzig (October, 1813). In this battle, Napoleon's forces were less than half as large as those of his opponents, and, besides, some of his German allies deserted and joined the foe, in the midst of the fight. The retreat after the battle of Leipzig also proved most disastrous, for, owing to some mistake, a bridge was blown up before all the army could cross, and many were thus cut off and lost, a brave Polish prince (Poniatowski) perishing in the attempt to swim across the river.

The battle of Leipzig is considered one of the decisive battles of the world, because it put an end to the French domination of Europe. Thereafter all the German states, no longer subject to Napoleon, banded against him, eager and ready to join Prussia and take their revenge by invading France. In this patriotic German uprising, Jerome—who had already once been dethroned and reinstated—lost forever the kingdom of Westphalia. The Germans, flushed with their recent triumph, hotly pursued the fleeing French, greeting with joy the "German Rhine," which, as their national song, "The Watch on the Rhine," declares, they meant henceforth to guard faithfully from the stranger's tread.

The Campaign of 1814

Nearly all Europe was now against Napoleon, and his frontiers were menaced on all sides at once. He therefore made a desperate effort to recover the confidence of Catholic Europe by liberating the Pope and sending him back to Rome; then he made a treaty with Spain, freeing King Ferdinand VII. and renouncing the throne for his brother Joseph,—a treaty which did not, however, prevent the English from continuing hostilities on their own account in southern France.

The allies had declared that they would "enter into no treaty while a single individual of the French army remained in Germany," and that they had "no wish to make war with France nor to diminish its territories or its commerce, their war being with the emperor only, or rather with that domination which he had too long exercised beyond the limits of his empire for the misfortune of Europe." It was, therefore, to punish and awe their foe, Napoleon, that the allies planned to invade France. They entered at three different points, their forces all converging toward Paris. Thus Napoleon had to oppose three armies, each stronger than his own, and it required such military genius as his to face such a task. Still, no choice remained, in his opinion, for the only terms the foe would now offer were to leave France the boundaries she had in 1789. In his indignation at this proposal, Napoleon exclaimed: "What! Leave France smaller than I found her? Never! I have sworn to maintain the integrity of the territory of the Republic. If the allies persist in wanting to dismember France, I see only three alternatives—to conquer, die, or abdicate!"

Critical as the situation was, Napoleon, nevertheless, believed he could cope with it when he set out on his winter campaign of 1814. Before leaving Paris, he appointed Marie Louise regent, begging his brother Joseph to advise her, and presented his boy to the National Guard, who swore to defend him; then Napoleon bade a tender farewell to his wife and three-year-old son, whom he was never to see again!

Never did Napoleon show more activity and genius than during the campaign of 1814, when he accomplished wonders. In fact, had not the country been too drained of men to supply him with sufficient soldiers, and his generals too weary with the past twenty years of almost constant warfare to support him with their former zeal, he would have succeeded in either driving out the foe or in annihilating them. As it was, in one month he fought fourteen battles, winning twelve against great odds. But, whereas the Germans and Austrians were now inclined to offer peace again, Alexander insisted upon their continuing the war, saying: "It would not be peace; it would be a truce which would not allow us to disarm one moment. I cannot come four hundred leagues every day to your assistance. No peace so long as Napoleon is on the throne!" Thus Napoleon's former friend was now his bitterest enemy; and, urged by him, the allies, strongly re-enforced, pressed every day nearer to the capital.

Napoleon now devised a stratagem whereby he hoped still to win the unequal contest. He ceased to resist the advance of the allies on the capital, merely sending a small force to Paris to organize the citizens for its defense, while he and his main army prepared to fall on the rear of the enemy. Said he, "Let Paris only defend itself, and not one foreigner will recross the Rhine!" But when the immense armies of the allies came near, the empress, influenced by Joseph, fled with her son from Paris, thereby causing such a panic that the people, fancying themselves abandoned, thought of nothing save making the best terms they could for themselves. Only part of them could be roused to fight; and when they were defeated (at the barrier of Clichy) after a heroic struggle, Paris promptly surrendered, allowing the allies to make a triumphal entry into the city.

Several of the marshals, deeming the imperial cause lost, yet wishing to continue to serve France, now surrendered, thus crippling Napoleon, just when he was hastening to rescue Paris! As what was already done could not be undone, the emperor retreated in despair to Fontainebleau, where he wished to make a last stand, but where his officers, weary of fighting, and hopeless of success, refused to strike another blow. Abandoned by all, yet hoping to induce his father-in-law to use his influence in behalf of the King of Rome, Napoleon wrote him the following letter:

"The Allied Powers having proclaimed the Emperor Napoleon as the sole obstacle to the reestablishment of peace in Europe, the Emperor Napoleon, faithful to his oath, declares that he is ready to descend from the throne, to quit France, and even to relinquish life, for the good of the country, which is inseparable from the rights of his son, from those of the Regency in the person of the Empress, and from the maintenance of the laws of the Empire.

Done at our Palace of Fontainebleau, April 4th, 1814.

But this renunciation came too late, for the Senate had already declared the Empire at an end, and freed the people from their oath of fidelity to its government. It fell to Ney's lot to crush Napoleon's last illusions, and he did so by telling him, France, the army, and the cause of peace demand an unconditional abdication!" Thus driven to bay, Napoleon signed (on the small round table still carefully preserved at Fontainebleau) the complete abdication that was demanded, and then sank into a state of brooding despair, from which some one compassionately tried to rouse him by saying how much his generals and army would miss him, to which remark he bitterly retorted: "Not at all! They will say, 'Ouf! Now we are going to rest!'"

Meantime, the allies had marched triumphantly into Paris—just as Napoleon had entered the majority of the capitals of Europe—and had been influenced by Talleyrand and other Royalists to ignore the claims of Napoleon's son, and recall the Bourbon dynasty to the French throne. So all the emblems of the Empire were hastily destroyed or transformed into royal ones,—the conventional bees into fleurs-de-lis,—and it was only with difficulty that some rabid partisans of the new government, and the Austrian soldiers, could be withheld from tearing down the Vendome column! You see, the tide had turned, and as the freedom of the press had been restored, the newspapers—long muzzled—now denounced Napoleon in unsparing terms.

Louis XVIII., who claimed to be "king by the grace of God," and dated his reign from the death of his nephew Louis XVII., was not, however, allowed to enter Paris until he had promised in the "Declaration of St. Ouen" to respect the rights of the people, who, taught by experience, demanded such a guarantee. His brother, the first to arrive, affably announced that with the restored monarchy all troubles would cease, the only difference being that "there was one more Frenchman in France!" He was closely followed by Louis XVIII., traveling slowly in the company of his niece, the Duchess of Angouleme (Madam Royal), for whom this return to France was fraught equally with pleasure and with pain, but who turned ghastly pale when addressed as "the Orphan of the Temple," and fainted on reentering the Tuileries, which she had left with her family under such tragic circumstances.

Farewells at Fontainebleau

Meantime, Napoleon was at Fontainebleau, where, after signing his abdication, he is said to have made a vain attempt to commit suicide by taking a poison whose strength was spent. The allies decided to allow him to retain his title of emperor, and to give him the island of Elba, with a yearly allowance of $1,000,000, while his wife was to have the duchy of Parma as long as she lived, in exchange for the dazzling imperial crown bestowed upon her at her marriage.

The usual sudden and cruel revulsion of feeling having taken place, Napoleon, the once adored, was now so execrated that elaborate preparations had to be made to convey him safely to a southern port. Before starting, Napoleon went down into the great court of Fontainebleau, to select the small force allowed to escort him to Elba, and to bid farewell to the remainder of his men. His parting speech was: "Soldiers, my old companions in arms, whom I have always found on the road to glory, we must at length part! I could have remained with you longer, but it must have been at the price of a cruel struggle; of the addition, probably, of a civil war to a foreign war; and I could not resolve to distract any longer the bosom of France. Enjoy the repose which you have so justly earned, and be happy. As for me, do not pity me. I have a mission still to perform, and to fulfill it I consent to live. This mission is to recount to posterity the great thing which we have done together. Adieu, my children. I would willingly press each of you to my heart, but I can at least embrace your general and your flag!"

After this dramatic and touching embrace, and in the midst of the tearful farewells of his men, Napoleon stepped into his traveling carriage and, escorted by commissioners sent by the allies, made his way southward. In the days of his prosperity Napoleon had realized how fickle people can be, for he had said: "For my part, I know very well I have no true friends. As long as I continue what I am, I may have as many friends as I please." But even he had no conception of what people could say and do to a fallen idol. The farther Napoleon proceeded, the more excited he found the people; and at Aix thousands were ready to stone him when he passed! To enable him to escape such violence, and to spare *him some of the cruel jibe's and insults, the commissioners disguised Napoleon as an Austrian officer for a time, and made haste to reach the port whence they set sail for Elba.

On first beholding his island empire, Napoleon ruefully exclaimed, "You must acknowledge that my island is pretty small!" It was, indeed, restricted space for one who had been master of nearly all Europe, and who had further aimed to become master of the world. Still, Napoleon entered his new realm cheerfully, and immediately set to work to reorganize and improve it, so as to make, it a model of its kind, keeping the while, as he expressed it, "an eye on France and on the Bourbons." He was, besides, very busy preparing a suitable home for his wife and child, whom he expected in the fall, but who were now visiting the Emperor of Austria in Vienna.

Meanwhile, Louis XVIII. was installing himself comfortably in the Tuileries, where many of the émigrés hastened to join him, expecting, of course, the highest positions in reward for their fidelity to the royal cause. Thus many changes were effected at court and elsewhere, and it proved very hard for some of Napoleon's tried officers to make room for men who had little or no experience in warfare, or who, worse still, had borne arms against France! Besides an unwelcome change of officers, the soldiers had another great grievance, which was the substitution of the white fleur-de-lis for the glorious red, white, and blue flag of the Revolution and Empire, and the suppression of the eagles which they had guarded so many years at the cost of their lives.

The old émigrés also did not hesitate to demand as a right the restoration of their former estates, and as most of these had been confiscated and sold since the Revolution began, their new owners were justly indignant at the thought that they might be dispossessed of lands they had not only paid for, but greatly improved.

The change of government from empire to monarchy necessitating a new constitution, Louis XVIII. sorely offended the nation by "vouchsafing" the Charter of 1814, which Frenchmen claimed as their due. Besides, his utter disregard of all that had been done, and of France's glorious history since his nephew's death, proved another grievance, of which people were constantly reminded by his mania for dating state documents "in the nineteenth year of our reign," and for closing them with the offensive old-time formula, "for such is our good pleasure."

On the 30th of May, 1814, the peace of Paris was concluded, which left France with the boundaries it had had in 1792; thus depriving her of some of the conquests made during the Republic and of all those made during the Empire. This peace also provided that Switzerland and the Netherlands should be independent countries, the latter including both Holland and Belgium; but as Napoleon had changed the map of Europe in so many places during his rule, the question how to rearrange it in Germany, Italy, and elsewhere was left to be settled at a congress to meet in Vienna, for which each power appointed delegates. The five great powers—Austria, France, Great Britain, Prussia, and Russia—and the many lesser states at first disagreed among themselves, because Russia and Prussia wished to enlarge their boundaries too greatly. It therefore took much negotiating to settle things, so that the congress was in session a long time.

The Return from Elba

The discussions of the congress of Vienna were printed in the European newspapers, which in time reported that many of its members were determined not to leave Napoleon in peaceful possession of Elba, but were planning to transport him, instead, to some remote place, as his presence so near

France and Italy would prove a constant menace to peace. This news duly reached Elba, where you can imagine how eagerly it was read and discussed. Napoleon was now very restive, not only because the congress seemed inclined to revoke the gift of Elba, but also because not a penny of the money promised had been paid him. Besides, his letters to his wife and son were intercepted and destroyed, thus showing that it was hardly likely that they would ever be allowed to join him; and he was constantly under the irksome surveillance of a commissioner sent by the allies to make sure that he should not leave Elba.

His sister Pauline, who had come to visit him, and who could journey to and fro at will, soon began to make frequent excursions to the mainland, secretly bearing many confidential communications, and thus enabling Napoleon to get in touch with his old friends. In this way, the emperor learned that the injudicious, tactless behavior of the Bourbons—of whom he was in the habit of saying that "they had learned nothing and forgotten nothing"—was alienating even their friends, and that French soldiers and officers, almost to a man, would welcome his return.

As you know, Napoleon was not a man to hesitate; he now began to arrange for a return to France, planning his measures with the same care as his famous battles, his own description of his methods being: I am always working. I think a great deal. If I appear ready to meet every emergency, to confront every problem, it is because, before undertaking any enterprise, I have long considered it, and have thus foreseen what could possibly occur. It is no genius which suddenly and secretly reveals to me what I have to say or do in some circumstance unforeseen by others; it is my own meditation and reflection. I am always working, when dining, when at the theater; I waken at night in order to work!"

It was necessary to act, however, before the congress took further measures to interfere with his liberty, so Napoleon took advantage of the brief absence of the allies' commissioner,—who had gone to Genoa,—to sail out of his Elba capital with the little fleet of fishing and merchant vessels always at hand. On these Napoleon had quickly embarked his small force, but it was only when the shores of his island were fading from view, that it became generally known on board that they were not making an excursion, as usual, but stealing a march upon the allies.

Then, while all the men who could write were below decks, eagerly making as many copies as possible of a vivid proclamation, Napoleon paced the deck with his principal confidants. While he was there, the vessel was suddenly hailed by an English ship, the captain asking, among other questions, for news of Napoleon. Taking the speaking trumpet from the astonished captain's hand, Napoleon personally answered this inquiry, laughingly wondering afterwards what the English captain would have said had he known who was speaking!

Without any hindrance the small fleet proceeded, and Napoleon landed safely in France with his handful of men. The proclamation the soldiers had

115

copied was now scattered broadcast. It ran as follows: "Frenchmen! In my exile I heard your complaints and your wishes. You blamed my long slumber, you reproached me with sacrificing the welfare of the country to my repose. I have traversed the sea, through perils of every kind; I return among you to claim my rights, which are yours." This proclamation spread like wildfire, making known every where the fact that Napoleon had returned; news which was welcomed by those who regretted him, by those who had grievances against the present government, and by the vast class for whom any change seems desirable and is therefore welcome.

Napoleon's march northwards began immediately, his ranks increasing rapidly as he proceeded. No one ventured to oppose him, at first, so the emperor could march at the head of his troop, calling out to the gaping peasants by the roadside, "Citizens, I count on the people, because I am one of the people!" To those who seemed to mistrust his former vaulting ambition, he frankly confessed that it had been a mistake on his part to try to make France mistress of the world, and he reassured all by speaking only of peace and order, with freedom of thought and action for everybody.

It was near Grenoble that Napoleon encountered the first troops sent to check his advance. Halting his force, the emperor advanced alone and on foot to meet them, unbuttoned his familiar gray overcoat, and exhibiting his well-known uniform, cried, "Is there any one among you who wants to kill his emperor?" These words, added to his magnetic presence, had the desired effect. The soldiers simply dropped their arms, and fell upon their knees, madly kissing his hands and garments and shouting, "Long live the emperor!" Then, drawing from hidden recesses in their knapsacks the precious eagles and the cockades of red, white, and blue which they had been treasuring so proudly, they showed they had not yet forgotten him or their glorious campaigns under his leadership. The fact that Napoleon actually recognized a number of them, and called them by name, recalling the scenes in which they had played a glorious part, helped to rekindle extravagant devotion for the beloved "Little Corporal," whom they again swore to follow everywhere.

A little further on Labedoyere brought Napoleon a whole regiment, and every town he approached welcomed him so warmly that not a single blow was struck. Everything promised to fulfill Napoleon's prediction to the soldiers, "Victory shall advance at charging gait, and the eagle, with the national colors, shall fly from steeple to steeple until it reaches the towers of Notre Dame!"

The Hundred Days

Meantime, Louis XVIII.'s brother and nephews tried hard to make the soldiers do their duty, but were unable to stem the tide. When the time came to fight, only one of the National Guards, it is said, remained faithful to the king.

Ney—now in the king's service—led an army southward, rashly promising to bring Napoleon back to Paris caged like a wild beast; but as he approached the district already held by the emperor, the example of other regiments proved so contagious that he and his army also deserted to join Napoleon. But one of his officers, eager to join the emperor, and yet mindful of his oath of fidelity to the king, broke his sword and regretfully left the ranks, saying, "It is easier for a man of honor to break iron than his word." After Ney's defection, a wag stuck up a notice on the Vendome column, purporting to come direct from Napoleon, and blandly bidding Louis XVIII. send him no more troops, as he already had all he needed!

At Bordeaux the Duchess of Angouleme made heroic personal efforts to induce the soldiers to fight for their king, showing such courage that Napoleon admiringly said she was the "only man of her family!" But the persuasions of the unhappy daughter of Louis XVI. proved of no avail; and the royal family—afraid of incurring Louis XVI.'s fate—fled in great haste from France, to the intense relief of Napoleon, who would not have known what to do with them if they had remained.

From Lyons to Paris the enthusiasm seemed to increase with every step, and when Napoleon reached the Tuileries, in the evening of March 20, 1815, he was borne up the grand staircase in the arms of his devoted adherents. He found many of his old officials already in their wonted places in the palace, and everything ready to receive him, in the rooms which Louis XVIII. had left only a few hours before.

This was a grand day,—the fifth anniversary of his son's birth,—and his friends boasted that a horse-chestnut tree in the palace gardens had just burst out in full bloom, as if to honor the occasion. In after years, also, his partisans claimed that this tree was always in bloom on the anniversary of Napoleon's return, although others of its kind might flower earlier or later, according to the season. Not a shot had been fired, not a drop of blood spilled, the flag of the Republic had literally "flown from steeple to steeple," so the change in government could be viewed only "as a conspiracy in which a whole nation was implicated." Thus began Napoleon's second reign, which is commonly known as "The Hundred Days," and which lasted from March 20 to June 22, 1815.

During his sojourn in Elba, where Napoleon had leisure to think dispassionately, and was no longer constantly surrounded by flatterers, he had perceived some of the mistakes he had made in his previous dealings with France. He therefore determined to rectify some of these past errors, and in earnest thereof appointed Carnot—a stanch Republican—minister of the interior, and granted full freedom to the press. He also declared: "I am not merely, as they have called me, the emperor of the soldiers; I am that of the peasants, of the commons of France. So, in spite of all that is past, you will see the people come back to me. There is sympathy between us, because I have risen from their midst. It is not with me as it is with the privileged class."

While Napoleon was reorganizing the government and army of France, his brother-in-law Murat who had hitherto been left in peaceful possession of Naples rashly laid claim to all Italy, but was defeated by the Austrians at Tolentino, and thus forfeited his crown, which was restored to its former bearer, who became once more "King of the Two Sicilies."

On the 26th of May, the new modifications in the imperial government were publicly announced on the Field of Mars, to the rapturous delight of the people, who registered one and a half million votes majority in favor of the restored empire. There, too, the emperor reviewed his new army, for, in spite of his openly avowed desire for peace, war was already near at hand. You see, the news of Napoleon's escape, reaching Vienna before the congress was dissolved, had roused the old coalition to new activity. The powers declared Napoleon an outlaw, and swore never to lay down their arms until he was punished. Some people even said,—for this time France as well as Napoleon, incurred their strictures,—"Let us march on to divide that impious land. We must exterminate that band of cutthroats called the French army. The world cannot dwell in peace as long as a French people exists!"

You can imagine the effect of such declarations upon an excitable people, justly proud of its past. Even those recently weary of warfare were now ready to fight again; and, had more time been granted him, Napoleon might perchance have armed all France, save the small Royalist region of the Vendee, which renewed the old civil war in favor of Louis XVIII.

Meantime, Napoleon's letters demanding the return of his wife and son had been disregarded, and he had not been allowed to communicate with them, so closely were they watched and guarded. He knew, therefore, that he could recover them only by awing his foes. Thinking that his best chances for success would be lost if he delayed action until the armies of the allies could unite, and anxious, besides, to carry the war out of the country, Napoleon decided to attack the armies of the English and Prussians stationed in Belgium, hoping that he could annihilate them separately before the Austrians and Russians could draw near France.

Waterloo

General Wellington, who commanded the English army, was at a ball in Brussels when the surprising news suddenly arrived that Napoleon was advancing. Quietly excusing himself, Wellington hurried to rejoin his troops, only to find Napoleon trying the old plan—so often successful—of driving the two allied armies apart, so as to overwhelm each separately.

The French army first defeated Blucher and his Prussians, with heavy losses, at Ligny, but did not succeed in routing them. Napoleon then sent part of his army, under Grouchy, to drive the Prussians farther away, while he himself, with most of his troops, made ready to attack the English army on the hill of Waterloo. He rightly felt that everything depended upon the result of the coming battle; and, although strangely depressed, inspired his soldiers as usual by a stirring address, concluding with the words, "Soldiers, for all brave Frenchmen the time has come to conquer or die!"

On the English side, those who had encountered Napoleon in battle before, were far more apprehensive of the result than Wellington, who declared, "I, at least, will not be frightened beforehand!" Like Napoleon, he knew that the whole campaign would be settled by the coming battle; for if he were driven back, he could no longer keep in touch with Blucher. When asked for instructions, therefore, he exclaimed, "Stand here till the last man falls!"

This battle of Waterloo, fought on June 18, 1815, was one of the most thrilling in history, and has been described so interestingly by great writers that you will like to read their accounts of it. There were brilliant charges and countercharges, and skillful cannonading, and through it all the troops behaved so well that Napoleon could not restrain the admiring cry, "How beautifully those English fight!" Still, they were even then being so hard pressed, that Wellington, knowing it would be impossible for his men to hold out much longer without aid, kept looking at his watch, and despairingly exclaimed, "Blucher or night!"

Meantime, Napoleon was hoping that General Grouchy might rejoin him after beating Blucher. On beholding troops in the distance, Napoleon joyfully concluded they were his own, and was thunderstruck on learning that they were Blucher's men joining his foe! The last chance of success was gone, although the French, exhausted by many hours of fighting, still made desperate efforts. Ney even surpassed his former feats of daring on this day, and at the end of the battle led a charge, crying, "Follow me; let me show you how a marshal of France dies!" But he did not have the good fortune to perish on the battlefield, as he wished: The Imperial Guards also distinguished themselves, standing and fighting to the very last, thus proving the truth of their general's boast, "The Guard dies, but never surrenders!"

When Napoleon saw that the day was lost, he, too, would fain have plunged into the fray, to die with his men; but one of his officers, seizing his horse's bridle, galloped away with him, and he thus became involved in the general stampede. The losses in this battle, where 118,000 foreigners were engaged in the fight against 70,000 Frenchmen, were enormous; and Wellington, gazing at the dead on the battlefield that evening, justly said, "A great victory is the saddest thing on earth except a great defeat!" All these dead were buried under mounds and in trenches, and the famous battlefield is now a military cemetery, where both the English lion and the French eagle serve as monuments to commemorate the brave soldiers who fought and died on either side on that awful day.

Realizing that all was over, Napoleon hastened back to Paris; and when his brothers urged him to make another attempt and "dare everything," he sadly exclaimed, "I have already dared too much." Knowing how few were willing to support him any longer, he abdicated a second time in favor of his son, saying: "Frenchmen, I offer myself a sacrifice to the hatred of the enemies of

The Battle of Waterloo - William Sadler

120

France. My public life is finished. I proclaim my son under the title of Napoleon II., Emperor of the French." Although the Senate recognized Napoleon II., thereby giving him a place among the rulers of France, their action was ignored by the allies, whose armies again poured into France for the purpose of forcing the French to accept Louis XVIII. as their master, and made them purchase peace at a high price.

Napoleon Deported

Although Napoleon had done great things for the country, his wars are estimated to have cost her about 1,700,000 lives. His foes had lost nearly 2,000,000 men, so all through Europe the name of Napoleon was hated by those who mourned these dead, as is vividly depicted in a painting (by Wiertz) at Brussels, representing Napoleon attacked, even in Hades, by a horde of revengeful furies, the mothers and wives of those for whose death he is responsible.

Meantime, urged to leave Paris lest his presence there endanger the city, Napoleon had taken leave of his family,—his little nephew Louis Napoleon (later Napoleon III.) clinging desperately to him, and had driven off to Malmaison, to revisit for the last time the gardens and rooms where he and Josephine had spent such happy hours. He also sought her tomb in the nearby village church (Rueil), and, last of all, entered the apartment where Josephine had died during his exile, her last words being, "Napoleon! Elba!" Taking leave of his step-daughter Hortense, he then started for the western coast, hoping to find there some vessel to convey him safely to the United States, where he meant to take up his abode. But as several English frigates were cruising up and down off Rochefort, he knew he would be captured and treated as a prisoner of war as soon as he got outside of the bar. Instead, Napoleon preferred to throw himself upon the generosity of the English, and therefore wrote the following letter to the regent of England:—

"ROYAL HIGHNESS:"

"A prey to the factions which divide my country, and to the enmity of the powers of Europe, I have terminated my public career, and I come, like Themistocles, to seat myself at the hearth of the British people. I place myself under the protection of its laws, which I claim

from your Royal Highness, as the most powerful, the most constant, and the most generous of my foes.

"NAPOLEON."

A free man, Napoleon stepped on board the *Bellerophon*,—an English man-of-war,—saying, "I have come to throw myself under the protection of the laws of England!" He was never to be free again, a fact which he must have dimly felt, for when the coasts of France faded from his view, he sadly exclaimed: "Farewell, land of the brave! Farewell, dear France. A few traitors less and you would still be a great nation, mistress of the world!" Instead of the home in England, or the United States, for which Napoleon had pleaded, he was transferred from the *Bellerophon* to another vessel, and conveyed, with the few faithful followers allowed to accompany him, to the island of St. Helena, in mid-Atlantic.

There, hundreds of miles from other lands, he was constantly watched and spied upon, and worried by the petty persecutions of his keeper Sir Hudson Lowe, whom we must say, however, Napoleon seemed to take pleasure in annoying as much as he could. But, accustomed to life in a palace, Napoleon was now lodged in a plain one-story building, where he was deprived of many ordinary comforts. Besides, sentinels posted here and there watched every step he took, until their presence became so irksome that the emperor finally preferred to remain in his room and small garden, rather than venture abroad and be annoyed by their proximity. During one of his few walks abroad, when one of his companions was trying to make a laden peasant-woman step aside to let the emperor pass, Napoleon climbed up on the rocks himself, to leave the narrow pathway free, saying, "Respect the burden!"

The most cruel feature of Napoleon's captivity, however, was that no tidings of his wife and son were ever allowed to reach him. So far as his wife is concerned, it was as well that Napoleon never had news of her; for she was faithless both to him and to her womanhood. Even while he was still in Elba, Marie Louise had ceased to care for him, and had fallen under the influence of one of her own attendants. When the Congress of Vienna finally gave her the duchy of Parma because she was the Austrian emperor's daughter, she abandoned her son to her father's keeping, and went off, perfectly happy, to live in the new home, where this favorite attendant became her prime minister and sole adviser.

But the little "King of Rome," who lost that title when Napoleon abdicated the first time, continued to mourn the father whom he could scarcely remember, and whom he had not seen since he was about three years old. His fidelity is all the more remarkable, because neither his mother nor any member of her family ever mentioned Napoleon in his presence, nor would they allow any one else to do so. Besides, the child was separated, almost immediately, from all his French attendants, and handed over to German servants.

Meanwhile there was nothing to make life tolerable for Napoleon. Tortured by inactivity, regretting the past, having no hope for the future, nagged by small discomforts and by a constant, galling sense of restraint, Napoleon further became the victim of a cancer of the stomach which caused him untold agony. It proved, therefore, a blessed relief when, on the 5th of May, 1821, after six years of captivity, Napoleon I. passed away. He was buried in a lonely valley, under a weeping willow, where his body was to remain some nineteen years before his admirers could carry out the fervent desire expressed in his will, "I wish my remains to rest on the banks of the Seine, amidst the French people whom I loved so dearly."

Since his death at St. Helena, Napoleon's fame has been steadily growing. The "Napoleonic Legend"—it is almost impossible to ascertain the exact truth about all the deeds of such a man—is so full of incident and romance that it has fired all imaginations. Thus the emperor still has the most extravagant admirers, as he certainly had the most bitter calumniators; but his enemy Chateaubriand spoke quite justly in saying, "The giant had to fall before I could measure his greatness!"

Ney Shot

Only a few days after Waterloo, the English and Prussians again marched proudly into Paris. They camped in front of the Tuileries, and all Wellington's influence had to be brought into play to prevent the Prussians from blowing up the Bridge of Jena, a lasting monument of their great defeats.

The next day, the Second Restoration was an accomplished fact, for Louis XVIII. reentered the capital, whence he had regretfully departed at the beginning of the Hundred Days, refusing to say farewell and predicting his speedy return. Talleyrand, whom the Prussians would gladly have blown up with the Bridge of Jena, now became prime minister, and immediately took all necessary measures to, disband the French army, to proscribe many of those who had joined Napoleon, and to arrange the terms for a second treaty of Paris.

Every day now it became more evident that even had Napoleon succeeded at Waterloo, he could never have maintained his position on the throne, for troops came pouring in on all sides until there were no less than eight hundred thousand foreigners in France. These immense hordes of strangers naturally made their presence unpleasantly felt; for all of them owed some grudge to the country which had dictated terms to them for so many years, only too often exercising her power unfairly.

Not only were the usual demands now made for money and territory, but each nation also claimed the trophies and spoils which Napoleon had carried off. Thus the Louvre, which he had made a storehouse of Europe's chief treasures, lost them again, and they were restored to the places whence they had been taken. The only objects not recoverable were the flags and military trophies which loyal keepers hastily destroyed, rather than let them revert to their former owners.

On coming to France in 1814, the king had pardoned every one save the regicides (those who had voted the death of Louis XVI.), but this time he felt that an example should be made of the leading traitors, especially of such military men as had betrayed their * trust. A proscription list of fifty-seven persons was therefore, made out, some of the victims being merely banished, while others were condemned to death. The first of the victims to be shot was Labedoyere, the man who had gone over to Napoleon with a whole regiment. But his companion (Lavalette) was saved from a similar fate by his clever wife, who, entering his prison in mourning garb and closely veiled, made him dress in her garments and thus effect an escape.

Ney, the Bravest of the Brave, who had proved unfaithful to his new master, Louis XVIII., when the growing success of Napoleon suddenly rekindled the devotion of years, was ruthlessly seized and tried, not by the usual military commission, but by a special court, which condemned him to death. It was while his wife was at the palace door, still beseeching a hearing, and still hoping to save his life, that Ney was marched off to his doom. Standing on the very spot where his statue can now be seen in Paris, he not only refused to have his eyes bandaged, but gave the final signal himself, saying: "Do you not know that for twenty years past I have been accustomed to look straight at bullets and cannon balls? Before God and my country, I protest against the verdict that condemns me. I appeal to mankind, to posterity, to God. Long live France! Soldiers, straight at the heart!"

The exile of Napoleon, and the execution of their idol, Ney, seemed unforgivable crimes to the soldiers, and many of them also resented the fact that Murat, who tried to stir up a rebellion in southern Italy in the hope of recovering his throne, was shot without being even granted a trial. Besides, in the south of France, where there were many Royalist centers, several of Napoleon's officers were lynched by angry mobs, and we are told that more than seven thousand Bonapartists were seized and banished, or imprisoned and put to death. This state of affairs, known as the Second White Terror, helped to keep unfortunate France in a state of ferment for some time longer.

Seeing that the Bourbons,—who "remembered nothing and forgot nothing,"—were making themselves very unpopular, Talleyrand cleverly made room for another minister, under whose sway the second treaty of Paris was concluded. Not only was France thereby reduced to the limits she had in 1790, but she was obliged to pay a huge war indemnity, and to maintain one hundred and fifty thousand soldiers for five years in frontier towns, in order to guard against further political changes. These conditions proved very humiliating to French pride, and the presence of the foreign soldiers became such torture that the French hastened to pay the last of the indemnity before it was due, and all breathed a sigh of relief when the occupation was thus brought to an end, two years sooner than had first been stipulated.

The restored government, under the Charter, was fashioned somewhat upon the plan of the English constitution, the two houses being called the Chamber of Peers and the Chamber of Deputies. But the king still insisted on "no compromise, no surrender," still called himself proudly "king in spite of everything" (le roi quand meme), and still persisted in ignoring the Empire, during which France had really reached its highest point of glory since the age of Charlemagne; all of which naturally caused friction and uneasiness.

Although Louis XVIII. claimed that "the reign of swords is over; the reign of ideas has begun," there were many of his own party who did not approve of his ideas; those, for instance, who were "more Royalist than the king himself," and the former Republicans whose reformatory and progressive work was being rapidly undone. Besides, the press was once more subjected to censure, and the schools were again placed under close religious supervision, thus inclining many to rebellion; so there were student and other riots, which all too often resulted in disorder and bloodshed.

Still, in spite of all these drawbacks, France was then better off than most of the other European countries, where not only the same spirit of dissatisfaction and unrest prevailed, but where the war debts were even greater; for Napoleon had cleverly made others pay for some of the wars by which he had brought France to her highest pitch of glory.

Death of Louis XVIII

To make more secure the crown of the Bourbons in France, a law was passed excluding all Bonapartes from France forever; but though in harmony with the king in some measures, the Chambers were sorely divided on other questions. It would be far too difficult to explain here the many political quarrels, and the numerous changes of ministers, in whose hands most of the responsibility of government rested; for, while the king was clever and well informed, he was far more a man of letters than of business, and had received none of the training necessary to fit him for the difficult task of ruling.

Louis XVIII. was a childless widower, far older than his years. His heir was his brother, the Count of Artois, whose eldest son, married to Louis XVI.'s daughter, was childless, too. Not to let the race die out, a marriage was arranged between the second son of the Count of Artois, called the Duke of Berry, and a daughter of the King of Naples; and it was believed that their children would in time be heirs to the French crown. The festivities of this royal wedding (1816) were the first in this reign; the king himself riding out in state to meet and welcome this new niece. Nevertheless, the honors of the Tuileries continued to be done by the Duchess of Angouleme, who was noted for her piety, the gravity of her demeanor, and a strangely hoarse voice, due, it was whispered, to her long and solitary imprisonment in the Temple.

Louis XVIII. was, besides, afflicted with the enormous appetite of his race, and therefore became so stout that he could hardly move. Each year this obesity increased, until during the last years of his life he never rose from the rolling chair in which he was moved from place to place. His brother, the Count of Artois, therefore had to represent him at court and military functions, and soon roused his jealousy by receiving the chief homage of faithful Royalists.

The birth of a granddaughter to this prince—a daughter to the Duke of Berry—proved a great disappointment, because the people wanted a son and heir. And about a year later, when the Duke of Berry was putting his wife into her carriage at the door of the opera, he was mortally wounded by an enemy of the Royalists. This assassin hoped that by thus murdering the only member of the royal family likely to have heirs, he would prevent the Bourbons from continuing to reign in France. Imagine, therefore, the delight of the Royalists when they heard soon after this that a son had been born to the Duke and Duchess of Berry! In their enthusiasm, they called the boy "The Child of Miracle," and the Child of Europe," quite as often as by his real title, the Duke of Bordeaux; and they even began a subscription to purchase for his benefit the royal castle of Chambord—then in the market. It is because they bestowed this castle upon him that this member of the royal family has since been known mostly as the Count of Chambord.

It was the year after this prince's birth that Napoleon died at fifty-one at St. Helena, his death defeating the hopes of those who had longed to see him return, and who had meanwhile been plotting and biding their time. With Napoleon I. gone, Bonapartists began to turn to his son, Napoleon II., who was a semi-prisoner at the court of Austria in his grandfather's charge. Still, this child of ten was a poor substitute for the man of genius who had made all Europe tremble, and no one was anxious to have any of his uncles govern France as regent, for none of them had shown political or military abilities. Napoleon's death at St. Helena, a prisoner, made a martyr of one who had already long been a hero, and the memoirs and letters printed by his friends, served not only to keep his memory enshrined in the hearts of Frenchmen, but to give him even greater importance dead than while alive and a prisoner.

After the conquest of France by the allied armies in 1815, the "Holy Alliance" had been formed, whereby the rulers of Austria, Prussia, and Russia (and later France also) pledged themselves to discourage all revolutionary ideas in their own lands and elsewhere. So when the Spaniards insisted upon having a constitutional monarchy, and the Spanish Parliament detained their king a prisoner, the Holy Alliance asked France to interfere in behalf of this Bourbon by sending troops into Spain.

The French armies, under the command of the Duke of Angouleme, therefore invaded Spain, entered Madrid, followed the Spanish army southward, and after taking the Trocadero, freed the king. It is in commemoration of this glorious episode, that the Parisians erected the Trocadero, a large building where popular entertainments are now given, and one of the many show places of their beautiful city.

Meantime, the king was becoming ever more infirm, and was falling more and more under the influence of those who would fain have had him return to the absolute monarchic system. On his deathbed, suddenly realizing that his brother—bigoted and impetuous—might make a worse mess of things, the king laid his hand upon the head of the young Count of Chambord, and warningly said, "Let Charles X. carefully guard the crown of this child!"

Louis XVIII. is the author of the famous saying, "Punctuality is the politeness of kings." He was the last ruler who died and was buried in France, where he had reigned for ten years without having ever been crowned. As soon as he had breathed his last, the customary solemn announcement was made, "The king is dead!" followed after a brief but impressive pause by

"Long live King Charles X."; for Louis XVI.'s second brother was now to mount the throne of France in his turn (1824).

Charles X

Charles X., kindly and affable, although very narrow-minded, was a true gentleman of the old school, priding himself greatly upon his conservatism, and saying, "Lafayette and I are the only men who have not changed since 1789." But when times change as much as they had in France from 1789 to 1824, it is anything but a merit to make no change in one's self. Charles X. so loathed the idea of a constitutional government, that he often stated, "I'd rather earn my bread than be King of England!" Such being his views, he aimed to become an arbitrary ruler, and, to reach his ends, did his best to win the hearts of the people by appearing among them in an easy, friendly way. Once he even thrust aside his guards by a graceful gesture, crying, No pikes!" to show that he felt no need of protection when surrounded by loyal subjects.

Charles X. first revealed how thoroughly he considered himself "king by divine right" when he arranged to be crowned at Rheims with all the old-time observances. For his anointment, it is said, the priests used the last drop of oil from the sacred ampulla, which was supposed to have been brought by a dove for Clovis's coronation. This vial had been ground to pieces upon the paving-stones during the Revolution, only one small fragment—to which still clung a drop of oil—being rescued and carefully preserved. Some Royalists now claim that it is because the *last* drop of this sacred oil was used for Charles X.'s coronation, that there have since been no more anointed kings of France.

Then, too, just as if the progress of science had not demonstrated the folly of many of the old superstitions, Charles X. claimed that, having been duly anointed, his touch had the power of curing scrofula, a belief which exposed him to the ridicule of all well-informed people. But there were other things which annoyed a progressive nation even more; for instance, the king asked for 200,000,000 to indemnify the émigrés for property lost during the Revolution. But, whereas this sum seemed far too great to those who considered that the nobles should have remained in France to guard their own interests, it seemed pitifully small to the émigrés themselves, who would fain have seen all the present owners of their family estates rudely dispossessed.

Then, too, Charles X. placed on the retired list many officers who had served under the Republic and the Empire, which sorely grieved the soldiers who had become attached to these leaders. Shortly after this, the king had a law passed punishing with death any one guilty of such sacrilege as robbing a church; and many people, believing that the changes they resented were mainly the work of the king's confessor,—in an effort to make the church again supreme,—began to murmur against the influence of priests in the government.

Hoping to stem the tide of criticism, and to gain his ends with less friction, the king further restrained the liberty of the press, allowing no books or papers to be issued unless they upheld his views, or at least did not oppose them. This narrow-minded tyranny could only injure his cause, and Lafayette shrewdly predicted what would happen, when he exclaimed during his last visit to the United States (1824), "France cannot be happy under Bourbon rule, and we shall soon have to send them adrift!"

Still, Charles X. could not help knowing that his rule was unpopular, for the Chambers now began to oppose him openly, and the National Guard clamored (1827), "Long live the Charter," and "Long live the Liberty of the Press," instead of greeting him as usual with cries of "Long live the king!" In his indignation at such behavior, Charles disbanded this force, rashly allowing each man, however, to retain his musket and uniform.

Soldiers and journalists were not the only men punished for expressing their views too openly, for the poet Beranger was arrested for writing poems about Napoleon and patriotic songs which were eagerly sung. Then, wishing to soothe popular discontent by trifling concessions, Charles authorized the formation of anew ministry, which allowed a little more freedom to the press, and put an end to the "black room system," by which private letters were frequently opened and read to ascertain whether the writers were loyal.

Meantime, the Greeks, weary of Turkish oppression, had been fighting for freedom since 1821. Their bravery, the cruelty of the Turks at the massacre of Chios, and the fact that Lord Byron lost his life in an attempt to help them, at length induced Russia, England, and France to send their united fleets, which sorely defeated the Turks at Navarino (1827). French troops then landed in Greece, whence they soon drove out an army of the Turks; and shortly after this, Turkey recognized Greece as the free and independent country she has been ever since.

Revolution of 1830

The Dey of Algiers having struck the French consul,—thereby insulting France,—a French force set out from Toulon (1827) to punish him. But, popular as the expedition otherwise was, it enraged the French to see it commanded by Bourmont, a general who had deserted Napoleon, and gone over to the enemy, on the eve of Waterloo. After the French fleet had bombarded Algiers, Bourmont easily seized it, finding there treasure enough to pay the costs of the expedition, and releasing many Christian captives held by the cruel Algerine pirates. This taking of Algiers proved the first step in the acquisition of what was to become the finest colonial possession of France.

Meantime, the situation had not improved in France. In a new attempt to revert to absolutism, the king appointed a prime minister whom the Chambers refused to support, declaring they did not approve of his views (1830).

To punish them, Charles X. again suppressed the liberty of the press, and dissolved the Chambers, at the same time ordering some unconstitutional changes in the electoral laws,—which proved the last straw.

On the morrow, notwithstanding the royal prohibition, the newspapers appeared as usual, printing their strictures so freely that popular excitement reached an intense pitch on the 27th, 28th, and 29th of July. The rage of the Parisians reached its climax when it became known that the king had given Marmont—the first of the marshals to desert Napoleon in 1814—command of the troops detailed to restore order in Paris. Hearing this, the disbanded National Guards donned their uniforms, seized their muskets, and hurried out into the streets, where they promptly erected great barricades, on top of which they planted the beloved red, white, and blue flag of the Republic and the Empire.

Attack of Algiers from the sea, 29 June 1830 - Théodore Gudin.

Meantime, the royal family were quietly sojourning at St. Cloud, deeming the disturbance nothing worse than one of the too frequent riots of the day. But serious fighting began in the streets, and finally some of the troops joined the rebels. Three days later, the Parisians had secured possession of the Tuileries, Louvre, and other public buildings, which they did not plunder or injure in any way, but above which they triumphantly hoisted their tricolored flag. It was the sight of this flag which made the king suddenly realize the gravity of the situation, and drove him first to the Trianon and then to Rambouillet, a few miles farther on. Here, finding himself deserted by all save a handful of faithful and mainly clerical partisans, Charles X. abdicated, as did also his son, the Dauphin, Duke of Angouleme, in favor of their grandson and nephew, the young Count of Chambord, whom they fancied the people would gladly welcome.

But this abdication came too late; the people had already placed Lafayette at the head of a temporary government, and had given the Duke of Orleans command of the troops. On learning that the rebels were advancing toward Rambouillet, threatening his liberty and perchance his life, Charles X. fled with his family to England, whence he afterwards went to Austria, where he died in 1836.

As Charles X. had, left the crown to his grandson, the Count of Chambord, the Royalists thenceforth persistently called this boy Henry V., although he never reigned. He was, however, the legitimate heir to the crown of France, and, as long as he lived, his faction hoped to see him at the head of a restored monarchy. When he died (1883), leaving no children, his rights passed to his cousins, the Orleanists, a branch of the family descended from the brother of Louis XIV.

During the brief period of the Restoration (1814-1830), Lamartine, Hugo, Guizot, and other writers (Delavigne, Beranger, Thierry) enriched French literature with poems, histories, and historic novels which are now considered classics; the painters of the epoch (Gericault, Delacroix, Delaroche, Ary Scheffer, Leopold Robert, and Ingres) are represented by masterpieces in the Louvre and elsewhere; and scientists (Cuvier, Arago, and Ampere) made invaluable contributions in their different branches of learning. During this period, also, the first savings-bank was founded, and Paris was embellished by fine buildings (the Bourse, the Church of St. Vincent de Paul, and the Chapelle Expiatoire). It was, however, just after this period that the famous July Column was erected as a monument to the six thousand victims of the Revolution of 1830—which is known also as the Second Revolution or the Revolution of Charles X.

The Orleanists

Believing that nothing could be better for France at this stage of proceedings than a real constitutional monarchy, with a king of the people's own choosing, the provisional government begged Lafayette to visit and sound the Duke of Orleans. Descended from the brother of Louis XIV., and eldest son of the abhorred Philip Equality, Louis Philippe had won the approval of the nation by fighting at Valmy and Jemappes for the French Republic. But since Dumouriez had lured him from the army, this youth had lived in exile, teaching school in Switzerland, traveling on horseback in the United States, and becoming a thorough democrat. Even after royalty had been restored in France, he insisted that his large family of children be brought up to attend the public schools, and become independent of circumstances by being fitted to earn their own living. Ever since the return of the Bourbons to France, this Duke of Orleans had lived in state in the Palais Royal, and, although not in sympathy with the government, he had nevertheless been received at the Tuileries as next of kin to the royal family.

Lafayette introduced his mission to the Duke of Orleans by saying, "You know that I am a Republican, and consider the American constitution the most perfect!"

"I am of the same opinion," promptly replied the Duke. "No one could have been two years in America and not share that view. But do you think that constitution could be adopted in France in its present condition, with the present state of popular opinion?"

"No," rejoined Lafayette. "What France needs is a popular monarchy, surrounded by republican—thoroughly republican—institutions."

"There I quite agree with you," said Louis Philippe.

As their opinions so thoroughly coincided, all preliminaries were quickly settled, and Lafayette himself presented Louis Philippe to the people, saying, "Behold, the best of republics!" Thus, on the 9th of August, 1830, the "citizen king," Louis Philippe, swore to respect the revised Charter, and, taking possession of the deserted Tuileries, began his reign as "King of the French,"—so called because he was chosen by the people.

Selected by the moneyed middle class,—the *bourgeoisie*,—Louis Philippe naturally catered to their wishes, allowing the real authority to rest mainly in the hands of such ministers as Guizot and Thiers. Although the Charter purported to be republican in nature, only citizens paying above $40 taxes were entitled to vote, so the ballot was restricted to some 200,000 voters, and therefore hardly represented the wishes of the whole country.

The very year after Louis Philippe began his reign, a demonstration was made by the Legitimists in favor of the Count of Chambord, the mob surrounding the Tuileries and breaking into a church near by. But this disturbance was promptly quelled without bloodshed, by using fire engines against the rebels, who scattered as promptly before streams of water as before grapeshot! Wishing to prevent his wife and daughters from hearing the rude remarks frequently made by people passing directly under the palace windows, Louis Philippe now had the street removed farther back, and separated from the palace by an iron railing, a thicket of shrubbery, and a deep moat. "My wife shall never be exposed to hear all the horrors Marie Antoinette heard there in the course of three years!" was his grim comment, for Louis Philippe was a much firmer man than Louis XVI., although no better husband or father.

Whatever France does is apt to be imitated by the rest of Europe. Thus the Revolution of 1830 inspired Poland to try—in vain—to recover her independence; induced Belgium to break away from Holland, with which it had been united in 1814; and led Italy to rebel—unsuccessfully—against the ever-increasing tyranny of Austria. In fact, people everywhere began to demand more liberty, so European kings hotly blamed Louis Philippe for every concession he made, while most of his subjects seemed to think he was inclined to play the autocrat. He had, besides, to contend continually with vari-

131

ous political parties in France; that of the Legitimists, who wished to place the Count of Chambord on the throne; that of the Bonapartists, who wished to restore the Empire; and that of the Red Republicans, or partisans of the old Republican system. This constant rivalry of parties gave rise to strikes, riots, and plots galore, as well as to several conspiracies against the king's life.

Belgium, having finally made good her independence,—thanks to the aid of the French and English at the siege of Antwerp,—offered its crown to one of Louis Philippe's sons; but the "citizen king," perceiving that an acceptance might cause jealousy among the other nations, declined this honor, which was passed on to Leopold. Still, it seemed decreed by fate that one of Louis Philippe's children should rule over the Belgians, for Leopold, being a widower, soon after his accession married Louise, one of the French king's accomplished daughters.

In 1832, France was visited by a terrible epidemic of cholera, which, starting in India, rapidly made its way around the globe, causing an awful loss of life. In Paris, where it raged 189 days, it carried off no less than 20,000 victims, but the courage displayed by the royal family—who visited the hospitals and stricken districts and took great pains to organize speedy relief measures—greatly endeared them to the French people. Among the victims of this epidemic was the prime minister Casimir Perier, one of many statesmen who helped to direct the government of France during this reign.

Interesting Events

Two events occurred in 1832, which will doubtless interest you, and which helped to strengthen Louis Philippe's position. First came the one which touched all the Bonapartists closely. You must know that Napoleon's son—called the King of Rome while his father was in power—had since 1814 been detained at his grandfather's court at Vienna, where he. was brought up as much like a German as possible, and was given the title Duke of Reichstadt. All his questions in regard to his father long remained unanswered, but in spite of the fact that he was allowed no French attendants, he remained devoted to his native country, and, being of an ardent, imaginative temperament, positively idolized the father he could barely recall.

From the first, Emperor Francis had discouraged all hope of his grandson's ever returning to France, and had guarded the youth carefully to prevent his getting in touch with the Bonapartist faction. So, although the Duke of Reichstadt—as he was now exclusively called—was given a very careful education, he never received any of the messages or legacies left by his dying father. He soon showed—like all his mother's family—tendencies to consumption; but, having chosen a military career, he deemed it a disgrace to shirk any of the duties or fatigues of his calling. He therefore so overtaxed his strength, that his grandfather had to place him under arrest in order to compel him to take the necessary rest. Even such drastic measures proved vain, as a rapid decline had already set in. So his mother, Marie Louise, was hastily summoned from her duchy at Parma to his deathbed at Schonbrunn, and saw him laid to rest in the ancestral vault in Vienna.

The death of "Napoleon II.," at twenty-one years of age, proved an awful blow to the Bonapartists, who had called him the Son of the Man," "the Child of Destiny," and "the Eaglet", and were merely waiting until he grew up, to attempt to place him on the throne, where they felt he would make a record for himself, because they knew he possessed more than ordinary intellectual gifts. By the death of the Duke of Reichstadt, Napoleon's brothers and their children became sole heirs of his glory; but, as we have seen, those brothers were not popular in France, and it seemed so difficult to make a wise selection among their numerous children that the Bonapartists' hopes now sank to a low ebb.

The second important occurrence of this year was a romantic attempt on the part of the young Duchess of Berry, assuming the title of regent, to secure the throne of France for her son, the Count of Chambord (or Duke of Bordeaux). Starting from Italy,—where she had secretly married a second time,—this lady centered southern France in disguise, met many Royalists there, and worked her way northward until she reached the ever loyal Vendee region. Few of the royal partisans, however, were ready to rise in her son's favor, and her presence and plots becoming known to the government, orders were issued to arrest her.

For a time, by assuming disguises, and by the devoted aid of her Royalist friends, the duchess managed to escape capture, but she was finally caught and detained in a fortress, until her second marriage was fully proved,— although she foolishly made a mystery about it. Her silly conduct caused so much ridicule that no one could ever take her seriously again in France; thus her rash and untimely attempt spoiled her son's chances for many a year, and strengthened the position of the Orleans family.

Three years later (1835), while the king was reviewing his troops in Paris, an Italian Republican attempted to kill him by means of an infernal machine. The king himself was uninjured, but several generals, soldiers, and spectators were killed or wounded. The author of this crime and his accomplices were duly tried and put to death, and new laws were made as speedily as possible to prevent such plots in the future.

It seemed, however, that Louis Philippe was never to reign in peace. In 1836, Louis Napoleon Bonaparte, son of Louis Bonaparte and Hortense, suddenly appeared on the bridge of Strassburg and made a speech to the French troops, claiming to be heir of Napoleon II.'s rights to the throne, and proposing to restore the Empire. By his sudden appearance and eloquent appeal to a glorious military past, Louis Napoleon won over one regiment; but before he could proceed any farther, he was seized by the police and borne off to Paris. Then, after a brief trial, he was contemptuously shipped to America, and bidden never to return.

The following year was marked by the marriage of the king's eldest son, Ferdinand, Duke of Orleans, and it was in honor of his wedding that Versailles—which had been set aside as a museum for the past grandeur of France—was first opened to the public. Here are exhibited the rooms and furniture used by Louis XI V., Louis XV., and Louis XV I., the coronation carriage of Napoleon I., and in a wonderful long gallery you can see pictures of the many battles in which the French of all ages have won undying laurels.

The fact that Louis Philippe's ministers secured a popular law for primary education (1833), under which public schools were organized everywhere in France, is one of the great glories of this reign. But the country was now in a thriving condition, and with increasing wealth and comfort, the people were able to demand education for their children. There was, besides, peace at home, although France was still at war in Algeria, and it seemed for a time as if she might become involved in the quarrels between the ruler of Egypt and his master, the Sultan. Trouble later arose with Mexico, but a French fleet under the Prince of Joinville, one of the king's sons, soon obtained due satisfaction.

It was during the early part of Louis Philippe's reign that Lafayette quietly passed away (1834). We have seen how this nobleman went to America to help the United States in their struggle for independence (1777). He returned home for a few months in 1779, but fought again in America until the surrender of Yorktown, and then, after five peaceful years with his family, made a third trip to the United States. Later, in France, Lafayette became a member of the States-General, commanded the National Guard during the trying period from 1789 to 1791, and helped found a club (the Feuillants). But while leading an army against the Austrians, he incurred the suspicions of the "terrorists" and was forced to flee from France. Although he took refuge on neutral soil, he was nevertheless arrested by the Austrians, and detained in prison five years. His devoted wife shared his captivity at Olmutz, while Washington vainly interceded for his release. It was not till 1799, under the Directory, that Bonaparte obtained the liberation of the man whom he contemptuously termed a "noodle," simply because he could not understand the lofty and disinterested—if not practical—motives which always ruled Lafayette's conduct.

After serving in the French legislature during the Hundred Days, and again in 1818—1824, Lafayette paid, a fourth visit to the United States, where he received a great ovation, the Americans not having forgotten the services he had rendered them. For the next five years he proved influential in the opposition party, and in 1830 again became commander of the National Guard during the Second Revolution. Having always advocated a constitutional monarchy, he was, as we have seen, glad to introduce Louis Philippe as king to the French.

Thus Lafayette helped make French history for about forty years, and played an important part in three revolutions one in America and two in France. He was buried in Paris, where his grave is often visited by Americans.

American school children have also contributed the money to erect a statue of him in Paris.

Second Funeral of Napoleon

Having distinguished himself in Mexico, the Prince of Joinville was rewarded by being appointed (1840) to convey the remains of Napoleon from St. Helena to France.

Although nineteen years had then passed by since "the Little Corporal" had breathed his last, there were still many veterans in France who continually talked about him, and the flood of literature in his honor had made every one familiar with his doings. The French, remembering how they had reached the highest point of their power during Napoleon's reign, now felt it fitting that his last wish should be fulfilled. So permission was secured from the English government, and all was prepared, not only for the long journey, but for a grand public funeral on the arrival of the body in France.

While the papers kept publishing Imperial reminiscences, Louis Napoleon, who had been living in London for some time, suddenly landed at Boulogne, with a few friends and a tame eagle, to repeat his rash Strassburg performance. But this time the soldiers, not carried away by his name or eloquence, promptly arrested him. Instead of being merely exiled, this prince was now locked up in the fortress of Ham, where he spent the next five years in solitary confinement.

On first hearing that he was not to be exiled, Louis Napoleon exclaimed, "At least, I shall die in France!" and when informed that he was condemned to perpetual imprisonment, he shrewdly inquired, "How long does perpetual last in France?" To pass the time he studied a great deal and wrote a book; later on he therefore often playfully referred to his advanced course in the "University of Ham." At the end of five years, taking advantage of the fact that many workmen were passing in and out while repairing the fortress where he was imprisoned, Louis Napoleon, with his servant's aid, cleverly disguised himself as a workman, and, carrying a plank, marched out of prison under the very noses of the sentinels!

Meanwhile, on the day that Louis Napoleon was arrested at Boulogne, the Prince of Joinville landed at St. Helena, where Napoleon's tomb was opened and the coffin lid unscrewed, so that some of those who had laid the emperor to rest could identify the body. To their amazement they still plainly recognized the features they had once loved so well, the body being remarkably well preserved. Conveyed to the waiting frigate, Napoleon's body was then borne to France, where it was enthusiastically welcomed, and taken in state along the Seine, under the great Arch of Triumph, down the thronged Champs Elysees, and across the bridge, to find a final resting place under the great dome of the Invalides. The funeral ceremony was most awe-inspiring, as is also the place where Napoleon now rests, surrounded by tokens of his glory, with his brothers Joseph and Jerome and some of his faithful marshals sleeping their last sleep only a few feet away from his sarcophagus.

Here Napoleon's remains were guarded by rapidly diminishing numbers of his veterans, who delighted in relating to visitors all they knew about "the Little Corporal," "Gray Coat," "the Eagle" some of the many nicknames affectionately bestowed upon him. In the church beyond his grave still hang many of the flags he won as trophies, fast falling to pieces, it is true, yet honored as the old tattered, blood-stained, bullet-riddled flags of the glorious First Empire!

De La Fosse's allegories under the dome over the tomb of Napoleon – Photograph by TheSuperMat

The fact that France nearly came to warfare with England, Russia, and Turkey over the Eastern Question, helped to determine Louis Philippe in 1840 to provide proper defenses for the city of Paris. Within the next few years, at the cost of some $30,000,000, the capital was inclosed—for the eighth time—in a new and more extensive belt of ramparts, a circle of forts further serving to strengthen its position.

While the younger sons of the king were distinguishing themselves in the army and navy, the eldest, most talented, and best-beloved, the Prince of Orleans, was making many friends at home, so that the French looked eagerly forward to the reign of so promising a prince, and took great pride in his beautiful wife and young son, the little Count of Paris, who had been publicly baptized in Notre Dame. But the object of these hopes, while driving out of the city one day to join his wife and children in the country, saw his horses suddenly take fright and run away. In their mad rush, the prince was thrown out on the pavement, and so seriously injured that he died a few hours later. On the spot where this talented young man thus perished, now stands the Chapel St. Ferdinand, containing his tomb, one of whose statues is the work of his artistic sister Marie; but his body rests in the Orleans mausoleum (at Dreux).

By the early death of the Prince of Orleans, a small child became the direct heir of Louis Philippe, and as it seemed likely that the king would die before this boy could attain years of discretion, the French began to dread a long regency. Besides, the deceased prince had named as guardian and regent for his son one of his brothers (the Duke of Nemours) who was so greatly disliked that this child and his cause became unpopular in France.

The country, however, continued peaceful for some years, both at home and abroad, excepting the war in Algeria. The pleasant relations with England were marked by Queen Victoria's visit to France,—the first time an English sovereign had landed in the country since the old days of Henry VIII. and the Field of the Cloth of Gold (1520),—and by a return visit of Louis Philippe and his Queen Marie Amelie to London. The friendship thus formed between the royal families of France and England was to continue even in adversity, when Louis Philippe sought refuge in Great Britain.

The Algerian Campaign

Just before the Revolution of 1830 and the flight of Charles X., the French forces under Bourmont, as we have seen, bombarded and seized the city of Algiers. The treasure this general seized and the slaves he freed make the story of this capture read like a romance, and the sorrowful departure of the defeated Dey, with a train of fifty-five veiled women, must have been picturesque in the extreme. Having seized the most important city of Algeria, the French decided to keep it, and gradually to extend their conquests; the result was an Algerian war that lasted, with brief intervals of peace, for some fifteen years. To carry it on, both men and money were needed, and, as many members of the Chambers were not in favor of the project, both were hard to obtain. This gave the French general the idea of enlisting and training native troops, and he thus raised the first regiment of "Zouaves", whose bagging Turkish trousers and bright caps (fezzes) attracted much attention, and were afterwards copied in the uniforms of some French soldiers.

The conquest of Oran in western Algeria, so roused the anger of the religious chief, Abd-el-Kadir, that he began in 1832 what threatened to prove a disastrous campaign for France. Blindly obeyed by his followers, very clever, and brave almost beyond belief, this chief proved no mean antagonist; still; the superior arms of the French got the better of his daring, for after two defeats he signed a peace, which lasted, however, but a year. Then the struggle was renewed, and a terrible battle took place in a defile, where, although at first victorious, the French could not long maintain their position. During their retreat many of these brave men were slain, their heads serving as ornaments for the pikes of their foes, who displayed these trophies with fiendish glee.

But, with new forces, and under better conditions, the French soon attacked Abd-el-Kadir again, destroyed his deserted capital, and again defeated him in battle. Then the French turned their attention to eastern Algeria, and, after failing in a first attempt to secure Constantine, made a new and successful venture with larger forces, until they became masters of nearly all Algeria.

Indeed, their only remaining foe was Abd-el-Kadir, who suddenly attacked and defeated a French army (1839), laid waste the French settlements, and kept large forces busy for several years before the country was reconquered: In this war the Orleans princes won many laurels. One of the most gallant actions took place at the fort Mazagran (1840), where 123 Frenchmen held 12,000 natives at bay for three days. The most picturesque episode, however, was the taking of Abd-el-Kadir's camp, where much treasure and many prisoners were secured. Abd-el-Kadir himself, surrounded by French soldiers, leaped his horse right over their heads, and escaped to Morocco, where he induced the Sultan to help him once more. But, after the French had won the battle of Isly, the Moroccans were ready to submit, and Abd-el-Kadir had to flee to the mountains. Tracked to a large cave, but refusing to surrender, one of his tribes was put to death by the smoke from fires built by the pursuers— one of Napoleon's old generals remarking, on this occasion, "What would be a crime against civilization in Europe, may be a justifiable necessity in Africa!" At last Abd-el-Kadir surrendered (1845), on condition that he should be sent to Egypt; but the French government, refusing to honor this, promise, kept him a prisoner in France for seven years, and then set him free on his agreement not to return to his native land.

Algeria, being conquered, has proved an important French possession, although there have been frequent clashes between conquerors and natives. The population, as a rule, is now loyal to France, thanks to whose protection the country is both rich and prosperous, and is rapidly becoming a favorite winter resort for invalids and tourists.

The Algerian war, lasting through almost all the reign of Louis Philippe, proved a source of great pride and interest to the French people, in spite of the great expense, although they have been accused of being at that time entirely taken up with the sordid desire of getting rich. It was during this reign, also, that France acquired her first interest in Madagascar, and that the first

French railways were constructed. Unfortunately, too many of these were begun at once, so that funds ran short before they were finished; as a result, the building of many lines was left to private companies, and the government now owns only part of the great network of rails that covers France.

Among discoveries of the time the most far-reaching was that of the scientist Daguerre, who invented the process since known as daguerreotyping, the fore-runner of photography. Then, too, the novelist and playwright Dumas, whose romances were to delight posterity, and who had begun his brilliant career as secretary to Louis Philippe, began to write his famous series of historical novels. But his literary work, however thrilling, is less artistic than that of Balzac, who ably and minutely depicted all phases of French character.

Among other writers who lend glory to Louis Philippe's reign, are the novelists George Sand and Victor Hugo, the poets Beranger and Lamartine, some noted essayists (St. Beuve and De Tocqueville), and great historians (Sismondi, Guizot, Michelet, Martin, and Thiers). Scientists also (Cuvier, Laplace, Arago, and Cousin) continued to enrich the world with their discoveries, and great artists (Vernet, Delaroche, Ary Scheffer, and Ingres) painted masterpieces to delight the eyes of coming generations as well as their own.

The Revolution of 1848

The main cause of the Revolution of 1848 was the displeasure of the people in general at not obtaining a better system of franchise, for which they had long been clamoring. The French people justly said that the two hundred thousand voters included only the rich class, and did not fairly represent the whole nation. In their eagerness to obtain what they felt was their due, the Republicans began giving public banquets, where speeches were openly made against the government. These banquets were permitted at first; but when they had greatly heated the people's imagination, an attempt was suddenly made to stop them,—an unwise measure which roused such indignation that even the National Guard now began to shout, "Long live Reform" instead of "Long live the King!"

The minister (Guizot) therefore resigned, and Louis Philippe was just preparing to make some of the long-denied concessions, when a fight suddenly broke out between a band of armed rioters and the regular troops. A score or more of the rioters having been killed, the mob paraded their bodies around the city, uttering rabid cries of "Vengeance!" Then Paris rose up in wrath; in the course of the next night, many of the streets were blocked with barricades, hastily constructed from uptorn paving-stones, or any other material upon which the rioters could lay hands. Each of these barricades was patrolled by rebels, who challenged all who attempted to go by, uttering bloodthirsty threats against those who happened not to share their political views.

The next day a raging, howling mob surrounded the Tuileries, and Louis Philippe, thinking his chances gone, hastily abdicated in favor of his grandson, and fled with his wife, mournfully repeating, "Just like Charles X.! Just like Charles X.!" The widowed Duchess of Orleans, afraid to remain in the palace, where she and her two small sons were in danger, hurried off with them to the Chamber, to have the Count of Paris recognized king, in Louis Philippe's stead. But the mob had already invaded and dissolved this Chamber, and had established a provisional government under seven prominent men, who were consulting at the city hall. Finding it impossible to return to the palace,—into which the mob had meanwhile broken, and where a ghastly scene of riot and pillage was taking place,—the Duchess of Orleans also fled to England with her two children. Her eldest son, the Count of Paris, now became the Orleanist Pretender, just as the Count of Chambord was the Legitimist Pretender, and Louis Napoleon the Bonapartist Pretender; all three, of course, claiming the throne of France.

To pacify the mob clamoring around the city hall, Lamartine—a member of the provisional government, and a great orator as well as a poet and writer—suddenly appeared on a balcony, and asked, "What do you want?"

"Your head!" howled a rioter, who evidently did not approve of this eminent author.

"I only wish you all had it on your shoulders, then you would show more sense!" retorted Lamartine, fearlessly,—a truth which struck home, and so amused the crowd that they became good-natured and more tractable. When they next demanded the "red flag of the Revolution," instead of the tricolor, Lamartine ended their hopes then and there by declaring, For my part, I shall never adopt it, for the tricolored flag has gone round the world during the Republic and Empire with your liberties and glory, while the red flag has merely gone round the Field of Mars, dragged in streams of blood from the people!"

The mob, having failed to institute anarchy and communism as they proposed, were glad to accept, with the rest of the people, a temporary government which gave all citizens over twenty-one the right of voting, and which assured freedom to everybody, even in the colonies. Elections were held almost immediately, for members of a National Assembly which was to frame the constitution of the new Republic. This Assembly, being continually interrupted by the arrival of deputations with petitions for this, that, and the other thing, had to be protected during sittings by the National Guard.

Meanwhile, to pacify the laboring class, which was in great distress because most of the factories were closed, "national workshops" had been organized, promising employment and fair wages to every one. But as the government did not have the necessary capital to keep this up any length of time, these workshops, after still further injuring business, had to be closed. In their rage, the unemployed workmen—some of whom had come from other parts of the country—began civil war in the streets of the capital, and kept up the fight until several thousand lives were lost. Even the venerable archbishop fell under the rioters' bullets, as he was trying to prevent further bloodshed by inducing the mob leaders to submit.

During these troubles, General Cavaignac was military dictator of the city, and he was then continued as chief executive until a new constitution was framed. This constitution of 1848 gave the chief power to a Legislative Assembly, with limited authority to a president, to be elected for one term only of four years. Cavaignac received 1,400,000 votes for president; but Louis Napoleon, who had returned to France soon after the Republic was proclaimed, received 5,400,000 and thus became first president of the Second Republic. His two attempts at Strassburg and Boulogne, and his romantic escape from Ham, had made him known everywhere, and the people believed him when he confidently asserted, "My name is a symbol of order, nationality, and glory!"

The new President and Assembly scored a first success and won the approval of loyal Catholics by sending French troops to Rome, where Italians in favor of a republic had deprived Pope Pius VII. of all temporal power (1849). Reinstated by the French troops, the Pope asked them to remain in Rome, and so it happened that the temporal power of the Popes was defended by French soldiers until 1870.

Another popular measure was the improvement of the law for primary education, while a highly unpopular change was a new restriction imposed upon voters, which withdrew the suffrage from nearly half the people. Besides, many people had accepted the new government merely as a step to tide the country over to the point they wished to reach, so there was little hope that it would long continue.

Meanwhile, the "Prince-President" had his own private ambitions, too, and to carry them out caused the secret arrest of his main opponents, illegally dissolved the Assembly, and insured quick compliance with his wishes by calling out the troops to put down all who resisted! After this *coup d'etat* (1851) he secured the adoption, by vote of all the people, of a new constitution giving him the presidency of the Republic for a term of ten years, with powers so extended that he possessed all the authority of a dictator. But this, too, proved only a step to higher position still, as Louis Napoleon soon persuaded the people that "the Empire is peace," and induced them to make him "Napoleon III., Emperor of the French" (1852).

The Second Empire was proclaimed in the castle of St. Cloud, where the first had begun forty-eight years before. As in the Empire of Napoleon I., also, there was to be a Legislative Corps and a Senate, but they were completely under the domination of the emperor.

The Second Empire

Having been proclaimed emperor, Napoleon III., like his model and predecessor, transformed into marshals all the generals who had best served his interests, and then began to hold court, not only at St. Cloud and the Tuileries, but also at Fontainebleau and Compiegne, where he often went to hunt. It was not, however, enough to be emperor himself; believing that the succession to the throne, and the future of France, should be assured, the bachelor emperor determined to marry. Because he realized that his proposals might not be accepted at foreign courts, he decided to marry the lady of his choice, instead of a princess, and proposed to Eugenie de Montijo, a lady of Spanish and French descent, noted for her grace and beauty. She immediately won the hearts of the French people by generously applying the money voted for wedding gifts, to the foundation of a popular charitable institution.

The imperial wedding in Notre Dame (1853), and the festivities connected with it, greatly delighted the Parisians, while the provincials were honored by seeing the imperial couple during the many journeys of inspection that the emperor loved. These journeys were beneficial because they led to many improvements, the emperor himself, for instance, setting an example by expending large sums from his private purse for drainage and other valuable agricultural experiments. Not only was Napoleon III. determined to make France the finest and most progressive country in the world, but also to make Paris the foremost city. To achieve the latter object, broad avenues were planned, paved with asphalt,—material which deadened noise and could not be used for barricades,—with frequent squares as playgrounds for the people. The city was also provided with fine markets, various public buildings, and especially the finest system of sewers in the world. Besides, the park of Vincennes and the Bois de Boulogne were transformed into delightful pleasure grounds for a nature-loving people; and in other parts of France, the castle of Pierrefonds was restored so that every one can now behold a perfect specimen of the old feudal fortresses of France, and the city of Carcassonne was so artistically rebuilt that it now stands exactly as it was in the medieval ages.

All through Napoleon III.'s reign such improvements continued, and while they cost immense sums at first, they were productive of great good. They also gave employment to hosts of workmen, and afforded a safe and never-ending subject of discussion and conversation for idlers. The emperor keenly realized that such talk was far less dangerous than political discussions, for hearing once that the people were murmuring, he exclaimed: "Regild the dome of the Invalides. That will give them something to look at!"

Still, the fact that all was not yet serene in France was demonstrated by occasional bread riots in different parts of the country, and by attempts to assassinate the emperor. But, on the other hand, the French were intensely pleased because England had immediately recognized the Second Empire; and the friendly feeling thus created between the two nations caused them soon to become allies.

Although Napoleon III. had declared, "The Empire is peace," he did not hesitate to make war when he thought it to the advantage of his country. In the first year of the Empire (1853), Russia began war against Turkey, whereupon France, England, and, later, Sardinia sent forces east, to help the Turks defend themselves. You see, Russia was already so large and powerful a country, that these other European powers were unwilling to let her seize Constantinople, as the possession of that city would make her mistress of the outlet of the Black Sea, and thus permit her, in case of war, to send warships out into the Mediterranean to attack them.

As great stores of supplies for the Russian army had been established at Sebastopol, in the Crimea, the bulk of the French and English forces were directed thither with orders to capture that city, while an English fleet entered the Baltic to attack Russia also on the northwest. The allied troops therefore landed in the Crimea, won a battle on the Alma, and began an eleven months' siege of Sebastopol (1854-1855). During that time, the French and English troops suffered untold hardships, being exposed to cholera and all the diseases from which an army suffers in the extremes of cold, heat, and dampness are experienced.

As things were sorely mismanaged in the hospitals, the English

The French capture Malakoff fort – Horace Vernet

government sent out Miss Florence Nightingale, with a competent staff of nurses. This clever, benevolent woman soon brought order out of chaos, saved many lives, and was so adored by the sick, that they kissed her shadow when it fell upon them. Her unselfish example has ever since been an inspiration to all women, especially to those who choose nursing as their profession.

Early in this siege were fought the famous battles of Balaklava,—where English courage won undying renown in the "charge of the Light Brigade,"— and Inkerman, where French re-enforcements came up just in time to second and save their English allies. Shortly after the Sardinian troops had joined the Crimean army, the French, by a gallant charge, seized the heights of Malakoff, commanding Sebastopol; and thus determined the surrender of that city. The Czar who began the war had meantime passed away, and his successor concluded a treaty, signed in Paris (1856), which left Turkey its old boundaries.

In token of the friendliness between France and England, Napoleon and Eugenie visited London and were entertained by Victoria and Albert, who later on came to Paris and were honored by a great exhibition and especially by a gorgeous state ball in the Hall of Mirrors at Versailles. The same year (1856) was also made memorable to Bonapartists by the birth of the only child of Napoleon III. and Eugenie, a boy who was called Louis in the family circle, but elsewhere was known as "the Prince Imperial." This child proved a source of national joy and interest, the French closely watching every phase of his development; and as the Prince Imperial was a fine lad, and admirably brought up, he naturally excited great expectations among stanch Bonapartists.

The Italian War

After the Crimean War it looked for a while as if the government might turn all its attention to the many improvements which were taking place in different parts of the country. Many railroads were being built, not only in France, but also in other countries, and in 1857 skillful engineers began the piercing of a railroad tunnel through Mont Cenis, to facilitate travel and commerce between France and Italy.

The next year, however, all Europe was shocked by the tidings of an attempt to assassinate the French emperor and empress. While they were on their way to the opera one evening, an infernal machine exploded so near them that their carriage horses and several of their guards were instantly killed. To avert a panic, Napoleon and Eugenie bravely hastened on, so as to be in their box, in view of every one, when the accident became known. As they showed the greatest courage and presence of mind, they received a tremendous ovation both at the opera and on their way home, for by that time all the Parisians were out on the boulevards—fine avenues built on the site of former bulwarks—reading the bulletins and eagerly discussing the startling news.

At the trial it was discovered that the attempt had been made by some Italians, who claimed that Napoleon III. deserved death because he was not keeping the oath he had made as a young man to help Italy become free. Although severe laws were now made against such miscreants, the emperor knew that attempts on his life would be repeated, as one of the Italians plainly declared. Shortly after this the great Italian statesman, Cavour, the prime minister of the King of Sardinia, came to visit the emperor, and proved that the time had come to make war against Austria, so Napoleon again promised to help the Italians. The first sign of this alliance was a marriage between the Sardinian king's daughter and Prince Napoleon, son of Jerome Bonaparte,— which gave occasion for many popular festivities. Then, early in May, 1859, when war began between Sardinia and Austria, France sent her troops to join the Sardinian army in northern Italy. Here the battles of Montebello and Magenta were won by the allied forces, General MacMahon of the French army distinguishing himself so greatly in the last encounter, that the emperor named him "Duke of Magenta" on the battlefield. The French were now able to enter Milan in triumph, where they were warmly greeted as deliverers, for the Austrian rule, imposed by the Congress of Vienna, had proved most irksome.

The Austrians having retreated, the allied Franco-Sardinian army followed them to Solferino, where another great battle was fought, with Emperor Napoleon, King Victor Emmanuel of Sardinia, and Emperor Francis Joseph of Austria all present in person. As the allies were again victorious here, Francis Joseph accepted an invitation to treat, and met Napoleon to settle the terms later embodied in the treaty of Zurich. The result of the war, then, was that Austria ceded Lombardy, which was promptly annexed by the Sardinians, while Venice remained under Austrian rule as before.

The Sardinian king, Victor Emmanuel, now ruled over a much enlarged kingdom, yet felt dissatisfied because Napoleon III. had not continued the war, as he had agreed to do, until Venice also had thrown off the Austrian yoke. The Sardinians taunted Napoleon with not keeping his promise, "Italy shall be free from the Alps to the Adriatic!" but although many blamed him at the time, it has since become known that Prussia was threatening to join Austria after the battle of Solferino, and that peace was necessary to avoid the great danger of an attack on the northern frontier of France while her main forces were busy in Italy.

Next year, however, by an overwhelming vote of the people, the various other states of northern Italy, except Venice, were added to Sardinia; and it was then that Napoleon claimed and received his reward for the help that had been given by the French army. Sardinia ceded to France the provinces of Nice and Savoy, which had been taken from the French at the time of the fall of Napoleon I.; and thus the boundaries of France were again extended to the Alps.

The active operations of the Italian War had lasted but two months and a half, and as the French army won every battle, you may imagine how proud the nation was, and what cheers greeted Napoleon III. when he reviewed the returning troops at the foot of the famous Vendome Column. Even the little three-year-old Prince Imperial was present on this festive occasion and was exhibited to the admiring soldiers and Parisians in a tiny military costume.

The emperor and empress soon made a state tour through Savoy and Nice, going from there to Corsica, to unveil a statue of Napoleon I., and then to Algeria, which, in spite of sundry risings among scattered tribes, had meanwhile been progressing with marvelous rapidity. During this imperial visit the first railway was begun there, but for many years transportation and travel continued to be carried on chiefly by means of horses, mules, and camels, along the ordinary roads which the French were building and improving as fast as possible.

Two imperial wars were not enough for France, so troops were sent to Syria to protect the Christians there against the Turks, and to China to compel the Chinese to respect Christian missionaries, and to open certain ports to European commerce. In the latter war French and English again fought bravely side by side. After defeating the foe they retaliated for the murder of the missionaries by burning down the famous Summer Palace, a museum of Chinese treasures of all kinds; only a few precious objects being saved from the flames by looting soldiers. After entering Peking, which had hitherto been closed to foreigners, the victorious Franco-English army dictated a treaty (Tientsin, 1858) by which sixteen ports were opened for trade, an advantage long sought, but until then impossible to obtain from the exclusive Chinese. Besides, a special territory was set aside for European colonists, while Christian missionaries of all denominations were henceforth allowed to go anywhere in China.

In another expedition to Cochin China,—where missionaries had also been molested and trade sorely hampered,—not only were similar privileges secured, but France also obtained her first foothold in what is now one of her thriving colonies. But such privileges were acquired only after many lives had been sacrificed and much suffering had been endured by the French soldiers.

The Mexican War

In 1860, new treaties of commerce were made, many political prisoners were released, and some reforms were made in the army; for Prussia was growing ever stronger, and the politicians who look far ahead were already predicting trouble for France in that region.. Still, it seemed as if the world were rapidly growing better, as so many measures were being taken about this time to help the sick and poor. There were, for instance, a number of savings banks, orphan asylums, old people's homes, day nurseries, dispensaries, free hospitals, convalescent homes, trade schools, and the like; and sanitary improvements of all kinds were being made, many of these being suggested, supported, and superintended, or frequently visited by the emperor, the empress, and even by the young Prince Imperial, who at an early age was initiated in all good works.

In 1861, France became involved in war with Mexico, against which England and Spain also sent ships to protect their commercial interests, constantly endangered by the political disturbances of that turbulent country. The ships of the three nations seized two coast cities, but when the Mexican government offered to treat, England and Spain accepted conditions which France refused. The result was that France continued the war alone, and, after taking the capital, proposed that Maximilian of Austria, brother of Emperor Francis Joseph, should become Emperor of Mexico (1863). Napoleon hoped thus to secure control of an American dependency, principally because the United States was then weakened by the long Civil War.

But the majority of the Mexicans were far too proud and independent to submit to the ruler thus forced upon them, so they kept up a stubborn resistance. Besides, the United States government, as soon as the Civil War was ended, reminded Napoleon forcibly that, in accordance with the Monroe Doctrine, it would not permit such interference by any European power in American affairs. Realizing that he must either leave Maximilian to manage as best he could in Mexico, or else face war with the United States, Napoleon promptly recalled the French troops; and Maximilian, after a brave struggle, betrayed by one of his generals, fell into the hands of the Mexican Republicans, who shot him (1867). Meantime, Maximilian's young wife Carlotta—daughter of Leopold and of Louis Philippe's daughter—had gone back to France, to implore aid for the husband she loved. Her anxiety, and cruel disappointment when these prayers remained fruitless, drove her insane, so that she never realized the sad fate of her adored husband.

French troops had been stationed at Rome since 1849 to protect the Pope, whom Italian patriots were constantly threatening to deprive of everything save his spiritual power, their aim being to make Rome the capital of United Italy. Napoleon was opposed to any further expansion of Sardinia; but Cavour, encouraged by the gains already made, continued in his great task of trying to bring about complete Italian unity by diplomacy, while such patriots as Garibaldi and Mazzini were fighting hard to secure it. With a regiment of about one thousand redshirted volunteers, Garibaldi landed in Sicily (1860), and within a few months actually seized Sicily and Naples, whence he drove the Bourbons, so that King Victor Emmanuel of Sardinia could claim the Two Sicilies as well as northern Italy.

A few years later this popular monarch was able to rejoice in a further step toward the unification of Italy. When war broke out between Prussia and Austria (1866), Victor Emmanuel, still cherishing the old-time grudge against Austria, promptly seized this occasion to invade Venice as the ally of Prussia; but this time he did not prove fortunate in war, and might have paid dearly for his attempt, had not his ally won the great victory of Sadowa. England, France, and Russia—none of whom cared to see Prussia increase too rapidly—now proposed to mediate, so a treaty was signed whereby Venice was finally joined to Italy. By another agreement, also, the French troops now left Rome, but as the followers of Garibaldi soon tried to wrest the city out of the Pope's keeping, the French returned to the rescue. In 1867, therefore, the kingdom of Italy included all Italy except Rome and its vicinity, where French troops upheld the authority of the Pope.

About this time, France and Prussia came to the verge of war in regard to the possession of Luxemburg, which was finally made an independent state; still, the strain caused by this quarrel left lasting marks in both countries. As apparently friendly relations continued, the various sovereigns of Germany—as well as of the remainder of Europe—came in state to Paris to visit the great International Exposition of 1867, to witness the formal opening of the Louvre,—now finished,—and to assist at a grand review at the Bois de Boulogne, where a sensation was caused when a Pole tried to assassinate the Czar.

Next year the French were called upon to show hospitality to royalty in a different way, for Queen Isabella, driven out of Spain by a revolution, sought refuge in France. She was received at the frontier by Eugenie, who graciously bade her old sovereign welcome, and saw that she was comfortably installed in Paris, where she continued to hold her court, although in exile.

As Napoleon III. was now seriously out of health; he was not able to be present at the formal opening of the Suez Canal (1869), which had been planned by De Lesseps, a cousin of the empress, and was paid for chiefly by French financiers. This canal, a triumph of engineering skill, cost some sixty millions, and took ten years to dig. It greatly shortened the journey to India and the East, and effected important changes in Egypt, through which much of the commerce of the world now passed. Because it was so great an aid to trade, all the European nations were duly represented at the celebration in honor of its completion; but the beautiful Empress of the French was the guest of honor, not only during the trip along the canal, but also at the festivities at Cairo, where the opera of *Aida* was given for the first time, having been composed on purpose for this occasion.

It was partly because his health was affected, also, that the emperor decided the time had come to give the French people more share in the government (1870). Therefore, with the help of a new prime minister (Ollivier), he submitted plans for liberal reforms to the voters, who pronounced in their favor by a vote of more than 7,000,000 to 1,500,000. These changes made the imperial government less despotic, and laid more of the responsibility on the people themselves. But before there was a chance to see how this would work, a new crisis arose in the affairs of poor France.

The Franco-Prussian War

You remember, do you not, how deeply the first Napoleon's wars and cruelty had branded hatred for the French into German hearts? This hatred had been kept alive by glowing patriotic songs and other writings. Meanwhile, the French, forgetting all their own sins, remembered only that while France had been robbed of her natural frontiers by the Congress of Vienna, Prussia had constantly been growing larger. In fact, not only had Prussia gained by the losses of France, but in two recent wars she had also wrested territory from Denmark and several small German states, besides recently preventing France from acquiring Luxemburg. Now, the newspapers suddenly announced that the crown of Spain had been offered to a cousin of the Prussian king, who, everybody knew, was by far the strongest and most important of the German rulers, and who was working hard to bring about German unity by creating a new German Empire of which Prussia would naturally be head. With such an empire on one side of them, always ready to threaten their peace, the French naturally did not want a foe on the other side, too, which would be the case should a German become ruler of Spain.

So vehement a protest was therefore made, that the prince in question, rather than bring about war by accepting, quietly declined the proffered honor. The Germans now considered the matter settled; but the French, dreading lest it might turn up again, asked King William of Prussia—son of Queen Louise—to promise he would not allow the prince to accept this offer if it were renewed. This old monarch, on hearing of this request from the French ambassador, politely declined to make the promise, and mischief-makers interpreted his courteous refusal as a deadly insult to France!

The clever Prussian minister Bismarck, who wished war, colored the news of this occurrence to suit his ends; the "yellow journal" element in France demanded war; and in the French ministry, the ambitious Eugenie threw her influence on the same side. People differ on the question who was most to blame. However that may be, the fact remains that upon the strength of a fancied insult, such a clamor arose in France that the ministry declared for war, and the Chamber, in spite of the opposition of Thiers and a few others, who kept repeating, "You are not ready," ratified the declaration by voting the necessary supplies (July 15, 1870).

Since "the real author of a war is not the man by whom it is declared, but the man by whom it is rendered necessary," this war, so often laid to the charge of Napoleon III, can more justly be ascribed to Bismarck, who for years past had systematically been preparing for the conflict and scheming to bring it about. He had made his plans so carefully that Germany had a perfectly equipped and finely drilled army, ready to advance at a moment's notice, under the guidance of such able men as Bismarck and Von Moltke, not to mention sundry German kings and princes. The patriotic spirit, so long fostered by German literature, was roused to instant action the moment war was declared, and all the Germans immediately banded together to prevent a new French invasion.

Meantime, Thiers proved right: the French were not ready, although the general-in-chief had boastfully declared, "Not a gaiter-button will have to be purchased!" Ill-equipped, poorly disciplined, and badly generaled, about 240,000 Frenchmen were hastily dispatched to defend a long stretch of frontier, and to oppose three magnificent armies composed, altogether, of much greater numbers.

Napoleon III., although desperately ill at the time, hastened to the frontier to join his troops, accompanied by his fourteen-year-old son, who was to have his first glimpse of actual warfare. They left the empress in charge at Paris as regent, and departed amid cheers, although the emperor was already troubled with presentiments of coming evil, and not nearly so sanguine as his soldiers, whose battle cry was, "On to Berlin!" The French emperor was, besides, sorely disappointed in his attempts to secure alliances.

Having helped the English in the Crimea, and the Italians in Italy, and having declared war upon the greatest enemy of the Austrians, he had naturally hoped to receive their support in time of need, but all three nations now decided to remain neutral.

The first action of the Franco-Prussian War took place at Saarbrucken, early in August, where the Prince Imperial "stood the first fire," and part of the French army won a doubtful advantage by defeating a smaller number of the enemy. Two days later another French force was defeated (Weissenburg), and, the French lines being broken, nothing prevented one of the German armies from entering France. Then came two battles (Worth and Spicheren) where the Germans triumphed again, but at a fearful cost of life, although numbering more than two to one. In the first of these encounters the French cuirassiers made a gallant charge to cover the retreat of their comrades; but these defeats left the way clear for the advance of three enormous columns of Germans—numbering some 250,000 men—under the able leadership of the princes of Prussia and Saxony, and of the best German generals.

On the flank of these forces—which plundered the country ruthlessly while passing, through—there was a large French army under General Bazaine, who deemed it his duty to remain near Metz, while fighting several battles in mid-August, chief among which was the desperate struggle at Gravelotte. At the end of this campaign, in spite of great daring and heroic charges on the part of the French, Bazaine found himself, surrounded by Germans, in the fortress of Metz, whence he could not escape to help his countrymen. After a siege of little more than two months, Bazaine surrendered fortress, men, and stores,—a deed for which he was tried later on, and condemned to death as a traitor. But this sentence was speedily changed to twenty years' imprisonment, his family being allowed to share his captivity; then, after eight months of close detention in the southern prison where the Iron Mask had been so long captive, Bazaine cleverly effected his escape and went to live in Spain, where he spent the remainder of his life trying to justify in his writings what Frenchmen and Germans alike consider a cowardly surrender.

Meantime, another army under General MacMahon, ordered to go and help Bazaine at Metz, was attacked on the way thither, and took position near Sedan, to await re-enforcements. During the next day, however, the French were surrounded by much larger forces of Germans, and were forced to fight at a great disadvantage, partly because MacMahon was wounded early in the battle. Only one cavalry corps managed to cut its way out; the rest of the army was driven into Sedan and was compelled to surrender. So did Napoleon III., who, in spite of great suffering, had heroically kept on horseback many hours in succession. He now wrote to the King of Prussia: "Not having been able to die in the midst of my troops, it only remains for me to place my sword in the hands of your Majesty. I am your Majesty's good brother, Napoleon."

But he was not to be allowed to treat directly with his opponent; instead, he was met by Bismarck, who rode beside his carriage until they could alight and hold a quiet conversation in front of a poor cottage by the wayside. When all had been arranged, Napoleon met William of Prussia in a neighboring castle, where he was courteously received, and learned that he was to have the Castle of Wilhelmshohe as his residence while a prisoner of war. But, although the emperor was captured, the Prince Imperial escaped, thanks to the presence of mind of his tutor, who, seeing that all was lost, hurried the lad into a train just leaving, and whisked him safely out of France into Belgium. From there, a few days later, they proceeded to England, where the young heir was to rejoin Eugenie and grow up under her care.

Meanwhile, the general who replaced the wounded MacMahon met Bismarck and Von Moltke and signed the Capitulation of Sedan. The victorious Germans secured thereby 80,000 prisoners of war, whose loss left the road to Paris undefended.

The End of the Second Empire

Each report of a new defeat of the French army naturally caused great excitement in all parts of France, but especially in Paris, the chief center both of population and of discontent. When it became evident that the country had been launched, unprepared, into a war which could only result fatally, public indignation against the government became extreme. Without pausing to weigh consequences, the people, ascribing all the evil which befell them to Napoleon III., railed against him without measure. Then riots took place, culminating three days after Sedan in a violent invasion of the Chamber, where the "Downfall of the Empire" was proclaimed, and a Commission of National Defense hastily organized. Still, even in the midst of the general confusion, some voices were raised in favor of law and order, Jules Favre, for instance, managing to give the populace the necessary caution: "No scenes of violence! Let us reserve our arms for our enemies!"

By surrendering to the Germans at Sedan, Napoleon III. escaped the vituperation which broke out on all sides, not only against his government, but also because he had surrendered. The common verdict was, "An emperor gets killed, but does not give up!" and such was the state of popular irritation, that no one now dared speak openly in favor of the fallen ruler.

The Prince Imperial having been safely carried out of the country by his tutor, the poor empress-regent remained alone in the Tuileries, to bear the whole weight of the people's displeasure. At first, many of the officials had sworn by all that was sacred to stand by her, but the loss of 17 out of 120 regiments,—either shut up in Metz or surrendered at Sedan,—and the fact that no troops were left to oppose the Prussians advancing toward the capital, filled all hearts' with despair. The empress not being a Frenchwoman by birth, the people wrongly assumed that she could not feel for them, and unjustly accused her, besides, of having spent in personal extravagance the money which should have been used for the country's defense. The result of all this was, that even while Eugenie was bending every thought and energy to save the situation, a wild mob broke into the Tuileries, from which she had to escape through the picture galleries of the Louvre!

Cast adrift in Paris with her companion, with only three francs in her pocket, the empress, after vainly trying to find some of her friends at home, had to cast herself upon the charity of her American dentist, who cleverly got her out of the city and country where her life was now in imminent danger. On arriving in England, Eugenie was joined by her son, and hospitably welcomed by Queen Victoria, who, having been her friend in prosperity, generously did all she could for her in time of need. The ex-empress, therefore, took up her abode at Chislehurst, where Napoleon III. came to join her when his captivity was over some six months later.

Meantime, the Government of National Defense, dating from the 4th of September, 1870, had intrusted the government of Paris to General Trochu and had given the venerable Thiers instructions to visit London, Florence, St. Petersburg, and Vienna, in hopes of inducing some or all of the governments located in those cities to intercede with Prussia in behalf of France. But in spite of all Thiers's patriotic eloquence, no help was vouchsafed. The Prussians, meanwhile, continually advancing, surrounded Paris on the 19th of September, thus beginning a memorable siege which was to last nearly four and a half months, and to cause untold suffering to about two million people. But before this siege began, the Parisians had heard how bravely Strassburg was resisting a whole month's bombardment, and although they felt that their capital would probably have to yield in the end, they were fully determined to rival their sister city in courage.

The Siege of Paris

One of the first duties of the Government of National Defense had been to arm or set to work every man in Paris, and to prepare for a siege by storing up the greatest possible quantity of fuel and provisions. Thus the new forts and ramparts built by Louis Philippe were stocked and manned as promptly as possible, and the suburbs cleared, the houses and trees in outlying parks being torn down to serve for fuel, as well as to prevent their masking the approach of the foe.

After the investment of the capital, no news could reach or leave beleaguered Paris save by means of carrier pigeons or balloons. Thanks to photography, however, even a carrier pigeon could bring, in microscopic form, a whole budget, and it was by such methods that the imprisoned Parisians learned of the successive capitulations of the fortresses of Toul, Strassburg, and Metz, and of the continued brave resistance of Belfort. The fact that Bazaine had surrendered Metz with its immense stores and a force of 170,000 men, proved a staggering blow for the poor Parisians, who had hitherto hoped that that army might yet break through the Prussian lines and come southward to deliver them! Then, too, while sufficient numbers of Germans were camping all around Paris to maintain the strictest blockade, large hostile forces were overrunning other parts of the country, although heroic attempts were made to check them at Orleans and elsewhere. The war in the provinces was energetically directed by Gambetta, a prominent member of the national government, who escaped from Paris in a balloon after the siege began and joined his colleagues at Tours, which had been made the temporary capital because Paris was cut off from communication with the rest of the country.

Time and again the Parisians planned sorties from one point or another, always hoping to break through the German lines and thus get news, provisions, and aid for their beleaguered fellow-citizens; but all these sorties, made by untrained and often badly led forces, resulted only in intense suffering and great loss of life. Heroic attempts to relieve the capital were also made by new armies raised in different parts of France; but although these forces did win several insignificant victories, none of them succeeded in reaching the capital. In the end, the French Army of the Loire was compelled to retreat toward the west and surrender; the Army of the North was driven toward Belgium; and the Army of the East, on its way to relieve Belfort, was driven into Switzerland, where, that being a neutral country, the men had to lay down their arms.

At first, the Parisians bore the siege with all the good-natured philosophy which characterizes the French nation. Even the rich gayly put up with all manner of privations and restrictions, and all seemed animated only by the desire to display the purest patriotism. So, while the men of all ages and ranks of society were employed in the trenches, ambulances, machine shops, and manufactories of ammunition, the women were equally busy in all branches of hospital and relief work, one and all doing their duty with a courage which cannot be sufficiently praised. There were, indeed, more than enough sick for these volunteer nurses to attend, for the winter was unusually early and cold, and the unwonted privations and constant exposure in the trenches and forts caused an alarming increase in disease. The sick, therefore, together with those wounded in the constant fighting, kept the beds of the improvised hospitals constantly full. Almost from the first, fuel and provisions had to be placed in charge of certain officials, who portioned out rations according to the number of persons in each family. If you have ever noticed the thousands of market wagons, the long trains of cars, and the many ships or boats which daily bring provisions into a large city, you can imagine how it must be when such a center is deprived for more than four months of all such supplies! Then, too, as fuel was scarce, no gas could be made, the streets had to remain unlighted, and even kitchen fires were used only when absolutely necessary, and then in the most economical fashion. Lack of fresh milk—the first supply to fall short—caused the death of babies by the score, so that more infants died during that siege than men.

Soon, ordinary meat could not be had even at fancy prices, and although all the animals at the "Zoo," all the cab and other horses, and finally all the dogs, cats, and rats were devoured, the Parisians daily suffered more and more from the pangs of constant, gnawing hunger. Even the provisions of flour and other cereals became so low that, toward the end, bread was made from a queer mixture of bran, chopped straw, and the sweepings of flour mills, such as would not, in ordinary times, be considered proper food for common cattle.

The worst came, however, when the Germans, exasperated by the Parisians' resistance, and hoping to compel them to surrender sooner, began to bombard the city two days after Christmas. With their great Krupp guns, the Prussians could throw huge bombshells over the forts and ramparts, into the very heart of the capital, where each exploding missile scattered death and destruction over a large area. At first the awful whizz of those bombs filled all hearts with dismay, but even timid citizens grew accustomed to them before long, so that they went about their business as calmly as if nothing were happening.

This bombardment lasted a whole month, for it was only when the last outside forces had been disarmed or driven far away, when the government had been obliged to flee from Tours to Bordeaux, and when the last sortie of one hundred thousand men had again failed to break through the German lines, that Paris, having scanty provisions for only a few days longer, at last capitulated (Jan. 28, 1871). As there was no possible hope of succor, this was really the only thing to do. The terms were arranged by Favre, who was sent out to Versailles under a flag of truce, to discuss matters with Bismarck, then cozily established in the royal palace built by Louis XIV. This was now, however, entirely occupied by the Germans, who, a few days before this, in the great Hall of Mirrors, had proclaimed King William of Prussia as Emperor of all Germany, the unification of that country having been hastened by this very war. It was thus in the palace of Versailles that Favre—who had declared at the beginning of the siege that "France would yield neither an inch of territory nor a stone of its fortresses"—was obliged to pocket his pride, and humbly inquire what terms the Germans would be willing to grant.

After some hesitation, it was agreed that the seventeen forts around Paris should at once be handed over to the Germans, that most of the French troops in Paris, except the National Guard, should be disarmed, and that the city should pay a war contribution of $40,000,000; and, on the other hand, a three weeks' truce was declared, in effect throughout all France, to give opportunity for the election of a National Assembly, which should decide whether to resume the war or to make a treaty of peace. Bismarck, however, refused to tell what terms he would demand in the final treaty.

It was with a heart filled with dark forebodings that Favre returned to the capital, to confess what he had done. To his surprise, however, the news of the armistice was received at first with joy by most of the Parisians, to whom it meant only that the siege and famine were over, that provisions and tidings could enter the city once more, and that many of them could join their families and friends who had gone elsewhere before the blockade began.

The Commune

Gambetta protested against an armistice made without consulting him, but he did not reject it. He urged the people to spend the three weeks' time in raising new forces to continue the war. The elections were held early in February, and the members elected betook themselves immediately to Bordeaux, where the people received Thiers—one of the successful candidates—with the imploring cry, "Thiers, get us out of this!" Nearly all the members were in favor of peace.

In this Assembly it was settled, by what is known as the "Bordeaux Compact," that first of all order must be restored in France, and the country freed from the German invader. Whether France should be in future a republic, a kingdom, or an empire, was not to be decided until later. Thiers, the ablest man present, begged the other deputies to subscribe to this compact, and was unanimously chosen to act meanwhile as the head of the government.

After appointing a minister, Thiers himself, with Favre, hastened to Versailles to secure the best terms possible from the victorious enemy. Bismarck, who carried on all the negotiations for the Germans, proved a very hard antagonist. He insisted, in the peace of Versailles, that France cede all Alsace and part of Lorraine to Germany, that an indemnity of $1,000,000,000 be given within three years' time, and that, until it was all paid, German troops should be quartered in France as security. It was also agreed that German troops might enter Paris in triumph, and occupy part of the city until the National Assembly should ratify the treaty. Thiers almost fainted when he heard the harsh terms demanded by Bismarck, but the only change he and Favre could secure was a slight reduction of the indemnity,—Bismarck's original demand was for $1,200,000,000. The National Assembly was to ratify this peace; and as the German troops were to stay in Paris till it did so, the Assembly ratified the treaty so promptly that the troops remained less than two days.

The "entry" of the invading troops was solemn and impressive indeed, for they came slowly marching along the Avenue of the Grande Armee, their bands bursting forth in triumphant airs under the Arch of Triumph of the Star. But Paris itself presented no festive appearance, the fine sculptures of the arch being still protected by boards, as during the bombardment, every window tightly closed, all the curtains drawn, and not one Frenchman either in the streets or up at the windows! 1 Down the deserted Champs Elysees the conquerors marched, before stopping and camping on the Place de la Concorde, for it had been agreed that they should advance no farther. The "line of demarcation" was guarded by double lines of German and French sentinels, to prevent any trouble. You can imagine the rejoicing in Paris when these Germans marched out again, the second day after entering, and the relief of Thiers and his government when this ordeal was safely over!

The Assembly was now transferred to Versailles, for Paris was still the center of the country and of the government. Meantime, the people there, relieved from famine by the raising of the siege, did not at first realize at what price peace had been obtained; but, having no work to do,—not even the guard duty which had occupied them so wholesomely during the siege,— they now had plenty of leisure to discuss matters. As usual, there were some men, who, meaning well but having little or no judgment, so wrought upon the mob by their eloquence, that popular excitement soon got beyond control. Then the entrance of the Germans proved "the last straw." Riots broke out with which the National Guard seemed to sympathize, instead of trying to suppress them.

Seeing the populace in such a state of ferment, the national government deemed it best to remove the cannon held by the National Guard, or militia of Paris. Infuriated by this attempt, the Parisians swarmed out against the regular troops, summarily shot two generals, and seized the cannon themselves! Whereupon, too weak to contend with the rioters, the government forces hastily withdrew to Versailles.

Thus left to manage as they pleased, these rebels took forcible possession of the city hall, and speedily organized a new government of the city of Paris, while the red revolutionary banner of the Commune was flaunted on all sides. The Commune of Paris not only denied the authority of Thiers and the National Assembly, but declared against the treaty of Versailles. Being utterly lawless themselves, the Communists could not, of course, maintain order; all wanted to lead, and all talked at once; one leader after another, therefore, was deposed as incompetent, while drunkenness and anarchy prevailed on all sides.

During the Commune, at the suggestion of a rabid architect, the mob undermined and tore down the famous Vendome Column, which soon lay prone on the pavement! Still, you will be interested to know that the architect was later punished for this act of vandalism, for when order was restored, he was condemned to pay all the costs of the re-erection of this historic monument.

The ignorant class, deluded into believing that all would soon be well, blindly obeyed the Commune, without perceiving that it was leading them straight to destruction. In their mad rage against Thiers for signing the Versailles treaty, they utterly destroyed his valuable historical library. The Commune not only disowned the government at Versailles, but would brook none of its interference; closing the city gates against it, and thus giving the signal for a new siege, for no decent national government could submit to the dictation of an insurgent city. Troops were therefore hastily collected to put down this insurrection, but only thirty thousand men were available, until the Germans, realizing the serious state of affairs, hastened the return of their war prisoners of Sedan and Metz. This army of about one hundred and fifty thousand, sent by the national government to subdue Paris, was scornfully termed by the Communists "the men of Versailles." When the Communists heard that this army was advancing to reduce them to order, they promptly seized as hostages some two hundred prominent citizens who favored the national government—among others the archbishop (Darboy).

The rule of the insurgent government of Paris, or "the Commune," lasted seventy-one days, and the second siege of the capital, which now began, continued during the last seven or eight weeks of that time. During this siege there was in Paris none of the law and order which marked the siege by the Germans. In fact, all good and peaceful citizens were terrorized by the violence of the mad rabble in command, who were just talking of a new Reign of Terror, and were proposing to set up a guillotine, when the government troops, after seizing several of the forts, succeeded at last in forcing their way into the city.

Seven days of grim fighting in Paris streets ensued, for the Communists had erected barricades everywhere, and madly defended themselves inch by inch. In their rage, they slew their hostages, including the venerable archbishop, and set fire to the Tuileries, the Louvre, and the city hall, besides many other important public and private buildings. The government troops, by rushing onward, succeeded in saving the Louvre with its art treasures, but the famous Tuileries are now nothing but a glorious memory!

Thus, although the Germans are to blame for ruining and sacking some places in the northeastern part of France, the Communists are mainly responsible for the awful destruction in Paris, where their name will always be held in abhorrence. To make sure that buildings once set afire would burn to the very ground, women of the lowest class were sent around to saturate them with kerosene, being on that account called keroseners. Many of these poor wretches were caught or shot down, in the very act of madly trying to spread the fire.

Rushing ever onward, the government forces brought the Communists to bay in a cemetery (Le Pere La Chaise), where no quarter was either given or taken, and where corpses lay strewn so thick, that "the air of the whole district was fraught with pestilence!" Besides the innumerable killed and wounded, the army of Versailles secured some ten thousand prisoners, a few of whom were executed on the spot, and others after trial by court-martial, while many were either exiled or deported for a number of years.

The Tuileries, destroyed by the Communists, and the palace of St. Cloud, set afire by French bombs to dislodge the Prussians during the first siege, have never been rebuilt; but the city hall has since been re-erected as nearly as possible as it was before.

Four Presidents

The new government having shown ability to cope with the situation by putting down the lawless Commune,—although at a fearful cost of life and property,—confidence was soon restored at home and abroad. Indeed, the story of the invasion of France, of the siege of Paris, and of the horrors of the Commune, had touched so many hearts, that contributions now came pouring in from all sides, thus helping the poorer Parisians to live, and the peasants to rebuild their ruined huts, restock their deserted farms, and purchase seed and tools to enable them to earn their living once more in their old homes. Meantime, the government in general, and Thiers in particular, were straining every nerve, not only to restore security and thereby prosperity to France, but also to collect and pay, the enormous war indemnity, without which the Germans refused to evacuate certain parts of the country.

Such was the patriotism of the people, however, that whenever a loan was called for, much more than the sum desired was immediately subscribed, and whereas Thiers had imagined that it would be impossible to comply with Germany's demands on time, and some people fancied it could never be done, the thousand million dollars were paid to the last penny on the 5th of September, 1873, and the last German soldier was seen to cross the French frontier a few days later! Most of the German soldiers had, of course, returned to their homes immediately after the war, and it is reported that Emperor William I., on his return, paid a visit to his mother's tomb, bending over to kiss her beautiful marble effigy and murmuring brokenly, "Mother, thou art avenged!"

When the arrangements for the last payment had been duly made, early in the spring of 1873, Thiers received an official vote of thanks from the Assembly, which enthusiastically declared that he "deserved well of the country," while the French everywhere hailed him rapturously as "Liberator of the Territory!"

Meantime, it was not only money that France had lost; the Germans had taken possession of Alsace and Lorraine, where German rule and the German language officially replaced the French, and was exclusively used in the schools. The inhabitants, however, were free to choose whether they would remain French citizens and leave their homes, or, renouncing France, remain where they were and become German citizens. This choice was, as you can imagine, a very cruel one, but many patriots lost everything rather than give up the right to call themselves Frenchmen, and the whole nation still mourns the loss of these two provinces, which have often been compared to two innocent little maidens borne off into captivity by a cruel foe! The statues of Alsace and Lorraine, or of their chief cities, are still veiled in crape on all festive occasions, thus showing that the wound bleeds on in spite of the years which have elapsed since the disastrous Franco-Prussian War.

The declaration of Thiers at Bordeaux, that when order was once restored the people would be at liberty to choose the government they preferred, had encouraged all political parties to help him, while biding their time, each faction of course deeming that it would be the one to reap the benefit of such forbearance. Very soon after the Commune, therefore, there was much agitation by the Legitimists, who wanted a monarchy with the Count of Chambord as king; by the Orleanists, who wanted the Count of Paris to head a constitutional monarchy; and by the Bonapartists, who wanted to restore the Empire. Each party tried to induce Thiers to favor its views, rather than uphold the Third French Republic, in which they knew he was, originally, no ardent believer, although he was now elected president.

Thiers, however, was shrewd enough to point out that while there might be one throne in France, he could see three claimants for it, of whom no two would ever be willing to allow the third to occupy it in peace! At first this argument seemed unanswerable, but the Legitimists, knowing that the Count of Chambord was already past middle age and childless, and that the Count of Paris was his heir and next of kin, hoped to induce the latter to forego all claim to the throne until the former's death. Then, after a vain attempt to effect a reconciliation between parties which had been estranged since 1830, some of the monarchists, fancying Thiers was the main obstacle to their success, succeeded in forcing him to hand in his resignation (1873).

On the following day, France unexpectedly found herself with a new executive, for, Thiers having resigned, Marshal MacMahon was immediately elected by the Assembly to be president in his stead.

MacMahon went to reside in the Elysee Palace, in Paris, thus transferring the government to the capital once more. A year later he formally opened the Grand Opera House, the largest and most beautiful theater in the world. To grace this occasion, the Lord Mayor of London and many other noted persons appeared officially, and were ushered up the grand staircase between lines of glittering cuirassiers.

The monarchists, knowing that MacMahon belonged by birth to their party, and the Bonapartists, knowing that he had earned his title (Duke of Magenta) while in the service of the Empire, both hoped for his support. A new attempt was therefore made—this time successfully—to end the feud between the Legitimists and Orleanists, so it looked for a while as if monarchy might after all be restored. In fact, the Count of Chambord graciously made many concessions; but when asked to allow France to retain the tricolor, to which the people were so attached, he firmly declared that he would never give up "the flag of Henry IV. and of Joan of Arc" for the "flag that France had chosen for herself." This obstinacy about "a napkin," as the royal banner was contemptuously styled by one great authority, proved to his long-suffering party that there would be no chance to restore royalty in France as long as he lived. As from their point of view a Republic was preferable to the Empire, the Royalists now loyally supported the government of MacMahon, even helping to pass the law (septennate) providing that the term of office of the French president should be seven years.

By a series of laws passed in 1875, during the administration of MacMahon,—second president of the Third French Republic,—the Assembly framed a new constitution which, with slight change, is still in force in France. The lawmaking power was given to a National Assembly consisting of two houses—a Senate elected mostly by the eighty-six departments, and a Chamber of Deputies elected by all the people. The National Assembly elects the president of the Republic (at Versailles), who appoints the ministers. The first elections gave a Republican majority in both Senate and Chamber; The fact that France had recovered with marvelous speed from the disastrous effects of the Franco-Prussian War, and that notwithstanding it had cost her some $3,000,000,000 she was not ruined, was demonstrated by a beautiful World's Fair, held in Paris in 1878, of which there still remains the magnificent building of the Trocadero.

The next year, although his term of office was not ended, MacMahon resigned (1879), whereupon the Senate and Chamber of Deputies elected Grevy, a Republican, third president of the Third Republic. It was in the beginning of Grevy's presidency that the Prince Imperial died in Zululand, to the lasting grief of the Bonapartists, whose hopes now had to be transferred to Prince Napoleon, son of Jerome, who was not at all popular, and who was best known by the derisive nickname Plon-Plon.

Taking advantage of some trouble with Tunis, France proceeded to invade that province (1881), over which she still holds a protectorate. From time to time, also, she gradually extended her authority in Madagascar, Tonkin, and Anam, although the wars in those regions, carried on in trying climates, cost innumerable lives and large sums of money.

Grevy, whose most noted saying is the oft-quoted, "I am here, I stay here!" *(J'y suis, j'y reste!)*, not only served out the full seven years of his first term, but was elected to serve a second term, just at a time when monarchists were holding up their heads with more pride because a daughter of the Count of Paris had married the heir of Portugal. Foreseeing trouble from their exalted state of mind, the minister of war (General Boulanger) secured a decree exiling all pretenders to the crown from France. But soon after, having become very popular, thanks to sundry army reforms, he was accused of aiming at military dictatorship, and for that reason was deprived of his command and placed on the retired list. This unwise measure only made a martyr and idol of this popular hero, whose praises were loudly sung everywhere. For no sufficient reason, many people expected great things of him, and at one time seemed ready to follow wherever he led; but, prosecuted by the government, he was soon obliged to flee from the country, and he ended his adventures by committing suicide.

Grevy, whose career had been most praiseworthy, was forced to resign (1887) because he rashly tried to shield his son-in-law who had been trafficking in decorations. The Senate and Chamber of Deputies thereupon elected in his stead Sadi Carnot, a grandson of the Carnot of Revolutionary fame. During his presidency, the one hundredth anniversary of the last meeting of the States-General was celebrated at Versailles (1889), and he opened an exposition (1889) which surpassed all its predecessors in beauty and extent, thus revealing to the world at large how fast France was progressing in every line. The Eiffel Tower is all that now remains of the glories of this World's Fair, in the course of which the one hundredth anniversary of the fall of the Bastille was celebrated with great popular rejoicings.

The Eiffel Tower in the final stage of construction, 1889

The Panama Scandal

France, as we have learned, had a large share in the construction of the Suez Canal, not only because its engineer was De Lesseps, a Frenchman, but also because French capitalists supplied a large part of the necessary funds to carry out the work. From the outset, the Suez Canal had proved of great benefit to the world in general, and to England in particular, whose road to India it shortened by half. The Egyptian ruler, believing that this canal, by bringing so much traffic through his country, was going to make it rich, became extravagant, planning and beginning many other improvements, for which he recklessly borrowed money at ruinously high rates of interest. The result of all this was that Egypt ran yearly deeper into debt, until it finally came to the verge of bankruptcy, in spite of the fact that it sold its shares in the Suez Canal Company to England for a very large sum.

As Frenchmen and Englishmen had loaned money to Egypt, the French and English governments decided to prevent their people from losing the money they had thus invested. Each government therefore sent a representative to Egypt, to regulate the finances of the country, and the Egyptian ruler, unable to extricate himself otherwise from his difficulties, reluctantly accepted their help. Later, from 1879 to 1882, a board of English, French, and Egyptian ministers practically governed all Egypt. But, although conditions were gradually improving, the Egyptians suffered so sorely from their past mistakes that they rebelled in 1882, taking matters into their own hands once more and driving both French and English out of their country! Although it had been settled that an Anglo-French force should put down any rebellion, the English, compelled to do all the fighting, denied the French any further right to interfere with the government of Egypt. Since 1882, England has therefore exercised a sole protectorate over Egypt, and has been the real mistress of the Suez Canal.

Meantime, having made money in one canal speculation, the French were continually urging De Lesseps to undertake another, this time across the narrow central part of America. De Lesseps having chosen the Isthmus of Panama as the most suitable point, a canal was begun in 1881 between Colon and Panama, which are some forty five miles apart. But, owing to the deadly climate, this proved a far more costly undertaking than the Suez Canal, and as De Lesseps was too old and too feeble to carry on the work in person, it fell into the hands of swindlers. They induced many people to invest, but squandered the canal company's money, so that eight years later the work had to be stopped for lack of funds before it was half done. As the canal company's stock was almost worthless, the French government made an inquiry to protect the investors (1892).

At first De Lesseps was accused of fraud, and condemned to a fine and imprisonment; but it was soon proved that his mind was too far gone with old age for him to have had any responsibility in the swindle, for which some of the real culprits were duly imprisoned and fined. But the fact that many newspapers, a few deputies, and even senators accepted bribes to misrepresent things, made the "Panama Scandal" one of the sensational events of the brief presidency of Sadi Carnot (1892—1894). This fourth president, proved a man of thorough integrity, and enjoyed great popularity until his career was suddenly cut short at Lyons by the dagger of an Italian anarchist (1894). As martyr-president he rests in the Pantheon.

The Dreyfus Affair

Carnot was succeeded by Casimir-Perier, during whose brief rule began the thrilling and mysterious Dreyfus Affair, which has been so much talked about, that it will doubtless interest you to hear a little about it. Alfred Dreyfus, an Alsatian Jew, officer in the French army, was one day suddenly and brutally arrested, without knowing what for. Brought before a court-martial, he was accused of treacherously selling information to the Germans, in proof whereof a paper was produced, which three experts out of five pronounced to be in his handwriting. This paper—not signed—had been found by a spy in the scrap basket of the German embassy, and was evidently the docketed outside cover of some document giving information in regard to secret military matters.

There has always been a strong prejudice in France against Jews. Besides, the French believe that the Germans were so successful in the Franco-Prussian War mainly because they were so well informed in regard to every inch of France, and as to its resources of all kinds. This knowledge, they claim, was furnished by traitors and spies, whom they have ever since been anxious to seize and punish. Almost instantly, therefore, it was generally believed that Dreyfus must be one of these base traitors,—although he protested his innocence,—a suspicion which seemed to be confirmed when, after a secret trial, he was condemned to be publicly degraded, and deported for life to Devil's Island, on the coast of French Guiana (1895).

Brought to the square before the military school, in the presence of five thousand soldiers, besides many newspaper reporters and other spectators, Dreyfus was solemnly told by the general in charge: "Dreyfus, you are unworthy to carry arms. In the name of the people of France, we degrade you!" Then the unfortunate man's sword was taken and broken, and buttons, shoulder straps, and stripes were roughly torn off the uniform he wore. Still, in spite of all this humiliation, the victim only cried: "Long live France! You have degraded an innocent man!"

Under strong escort, Dreyfus was borne off to the coast, and from thence to solitary confinement on an island, where he suffered not only from the unhealthful climate, but from harsh treatment; for his keepers believed him guilty of the basest of crimes. During Dreyfus's four years of martyrdom on Devil's Island,—he was once chained to his pallet for two months,—no news of his family, friends, or the outer world reached him. The government, however, insisted upon receiving a daily cablegram to make sure he was securely guarded, this little precaution helping to make his custody cost the nation some $10,000 a year.

Meanwhile, although Dreyfus did not know it at the time, the finding of more papers, in the same writing, in the scrap basket of the German embassy, caused General Picquart to suspect that all was not right. But when Picquart called the attention of his superiors to it, they treated him at first with contempt. After a while, however, the Dreyfus case came to the front once more, the writing this time being said to correspond exactly with that of another officer (Esterhazy). Three men—Dreyfus's brother, the novelist Zola, and a member of the Senate—now made great efforts to clear the matter up, but all they could obtain was a formal assertion from the War Office that positive proofs of Dreyfus's guilt existed. Still, when these so-called proofs were finally produced, the only important paper was discovered to be a mere forgery!

As the German and Italian governments testified that they had never had any dealings with Dreyfus, public opinion now clamored for a new trial, Zola being particularly active, and publishing a sensational pamphlet, in which he boldly accused court, war office, and government of rank injustice. On account of this pamphlet, Zola was tried for libel, and condemned to a fine and to a year's imprisonment. The latter penalty he evaded by secretly leaving the country, while his friends attended the government sale of his effects, and cleverly bidding against each other as they had previously arranged, contrived that the first object auctioned off—a cheap table—should cover the whole amount of the fine, thus, of course, preventing any further disposal of the author's property.

Still, the sensation caused by the trial of so prominent a literary man, eventually brought about the result that Zola wished,—namely, an order to try the Dreyfus case over again. While the victim of this mysterious plot was crossing the ocean to stand a second trial, another officer (Henry) confessed that he had forged the papers on the strength of which Dreyfus had been branded as a traitor. This officer was soon after found dead in his prison; where some claim he committed suicide, while others insist that he was basely murdered.

The new Dreyfus trial was held (1899), like the first, by army officers. Just at its most critical point, the prisoner's lawyer was shot at and wounded so seriously that for eight days he could not appear in court. While nothing was really proved against Dreyfus, the prejudice of the army against him was so great that he was again pronounced guilty, "with extenuating circumstances," and sentenced to ten years' imprisonment, the five spent on Devil's Island being half of the penalty. Once more, the prisoner loudly protested that he was unjustly condemned,—a statement which the president (Loubet) and his ministers must have credited; for he was shortly after pardoned and allowed to rejoin his family, a free man, although sorely broken in health and still bearing the stigma of traitor.

This "pardon," however, could not satisfy Dreyfus, who, as soon as he recovered sufficient strength, so successfully renewed his efforts to clear his name from the brand of treachery to France, that he was publicly reinstated in the army (1906), although he no longer had the strength to serve as a soldier. At the same time Picquart was proved to have acted so honorably that he was advanced to the rank of brigadier-general and two years later was appointed Minister of War.

This Dreyfus affair exerted a wide influence upon French politics, people vehemently siding for or against him, the army, and the government, in turn. But it now seems clearly proved that Dreyfus was unjustly accused of the crime of some other man, known and shielded by those in authority.

France in Our Day

Meantime, after a presidency of some six months, Casimir-Perier (1894—1895) had resigned, to be replaced by Favre, sixth president, who concluded an alliance with Russia (1895), and exchanged official visits with the Czar Nicholas II.

Loubet, seventh president of the French Republic, duly followed his example, but, before undertaking the long journey to Russia, he had occasion to entertain many distinguished visitors in Paris, where at the Exposition of 1900 there were ninety-seven million admissions. The permanent constructions remaining after this vast exposition are the Bridge Alexander, and two great palaces (Petit Palais and Grand Palais) where national exhibitions of all kinds are constantly held.

In 1898 occurred the "Fasho'da Incident" which, for a short time, threatened to occasion war between England and France in the Nile Valley. It seems that a French exploring expedition (under Marchand), starting from the French Congo, crossed Africa and raised the French flag at Fashoda on the White Nile. The English, whose protectorate over Egypt had continued ever since 1882, and who, were just completing the subjection of the upper Nile valley, strongly objected to the appearance of the French in that region, to which they claimed Egypt alone had any right. Fortunately, the officials on both sides behaved with such dignity and courtesy in this delicate matter, that affairs could soon be amicably adjusted by their respective governments.

Meantime, another dispute between England and France, regarding possession and trade rights in Siam, lasted three years, and was settled at last by making part of Siam neutral territory between English Burma and French Indo-China (1899).

Various foreign countries have always been anxious to get footholds in China so as to trade there. For a long while the Chinese, however, would not allow strangers to set foot in their country. Little by little this prejudice gave way, until five ports had been thrown open for foreign trade (1842). Many foreigners settled in these ports, while Christian missionaries, in spite of dangers and persecution, visited different parts of China to preach the gospel. Still, the concessions made by the Chinese did not satisfy the foreigners, who gradually gained more and more. The English and Germans proved so grasping, that a Chinese Religious Society, the "Boxers," began to plan in 1899 to drive all foreigners out of the country, so as to keep their old religion and mode of living and trading unchanged.

Because the Germans and English had seized ports in China, the French wished one, too, and when it was refused, simply took possession of Kwang-chau (1900). This deprived China of an important port, and as the foreigners everywhere had treated the Chinese unfairly, it decided the outbreak of the Boxer Rebellion. During this war, many foreigners missionaries and others were slain and their property destroyed. Even the lives of the foreign ambassadors were in great danger, for they and their friends were besieged in Peking two months, during which they were cut off from all communication with their governments. Such being the case, the foreign powers banded together, and their troops forced a way to Peking to relieve the besieged. Still, it was only after many lives had been lost, and much property stolen or destroyed, that the trouble was finally settled, and the foreign troops could withdraw from Peking (1901).

As you already know, France is a Catholic country; some thirty-six out of its thirty-eight million inhabitants profess that religion. During the Revolution, which was largely instigated by writers openly opposed to Christianity, the Church went down with the Monarchy, and all Church property was confiscated for the benefit of the State, while Christian worship was partly suppressed.

But after Bonaparte became Consul, he signed the Concordat with the Pope (1801)—an agreement providing that the State should pay the salaries of the Catholic clergy, and should have certain control over the secular affairs of the Church, the appointment of bishops, etc. This arrangement lasted nearly one hundred years, during which up to eight million dollars a year was paid by the State to the Catholic clergy. The State also paid Protestant and Jewish clergy proportionate amounts (up to four hundred thousand dollars yearly).

From the beginning the Concordat never proved entirely satisfactory to Church or State, but as Monarchy and Empire upheld the Church, the religious congregations gradually grew in strength and in influence, until they largely controlled charitable and educational matters, some 16,000 schools being in their hands. Since 1870, when the Third Republic was proclaimed, the majority of the Republicans have claimed that clerical teaching was against republican principles; as a result there was so much friction, that in 1901 the National Assembly decreed the suppression of the teaching and charitable orders, the confiscation of much property, and stopped all religious teaching in the public schools. These changes were not effected without protest and riots, and have in many instances caused great suffering to those whose lives they so entirely changed.

Previously we read how the change from Monarchy to Republic (1792) was not accomplished without harshness, injustice, and bitterness of feeling, because nations cannot change in a day the habits of centuries. You can readily understand, therefore, that this sudden change in time-honored religious habits caused extreme irritation. The interference of the government in the election of certain bishops finally brought about a crisis, and the party led by Clemenceau secured the repeal of the Concordat (1905).

Since then, the clergy in France have depended entirely upon the voluntary offerings of the people, such church buildings, however, as are not reserved for government purposes, being in the hands of local trustees and still used by the respective churches. This Church and State question, the most important topic in France during the first decade of the twentieth century, still causes trouble, although both parties hope it can in time be satisfactorily adjusted.

Meantime, some other things occurred which are worth mentioning, amongst others the eruption of Mt. Pelee, on the island of Martinique,—a French colony,—which in May, 1901, destroyed the city of St. Pierre and several villages, thus causing the death of some twenty-five thousand people. Not only did ruin spread over miles of fertile country, but the home of Josephine and her statue—which were the pride of the island—suffered greatly.

In 1902 the army law was changed for the second time. After the war of 1870 every young Frenchman had been obliged to serve five years unless he could pass a very rigid examination. In that case he could become "Volunteer" and serve but one. This requirement was changed in Boulanger's time to three years' service, and in 1902 it was reduced to two years' army life for every able-bodied citizen.

Louis Blériot in England after crossing the English Channel by plane.

In spite of the troublesome Church and State question, which kept the country in a state of ferment, Loubet proved so calm and able a president, that he served his full time, making room for Fallieres (1906), who, like his predecessors, paid sundry visits to European courts, where he has been duly honored as representative of France.

During the early part of the twentieth century, owing to the fact that neither pretender was popular, less and less has been heard of the Royalist and Imperial parties. So, at elections the main question now seems to be which republican party will get the upper hand.

During the last fifty years in France many famous names occur in every branch of science; literature, and art, some of which have already been mentioned. Were merely the names of the men and women distinguished in these different branches printed here, they would fill many pages. Still, many of you will read either in French or in translations, the fascinating works of Daudet and other novelists, the poetry of Rostand, and the plays of the younger Dumas, to mention one name only in each of these great branches. You will also doubtless enjoy the music of Gounod, and the paintings of Rosa Bonheur, as well as those of the many artists whose names appear under illustrations in this book.

There have, besides, been great physicians like Pasteur, who, you know, discovered a way to save the lives of many babies, and a cure for mad-dog bites if you take it in time; great chemists like Mr. and Mrs. Curie, and great inventors of all kinds. There are, for instance, inventors of airships there, who have done great things since the time when the first balloon rose from the lawn at Versailles, in the days of Marie Antoinette, until a Frenchman (Bleriot) was first to fly across the English Channel to England in a monoplane, in 1909, covering the twenty-one miles in thirty-seven minutes. Less than a month later he also took part in the flying matches at Rheims, where aviators of different nations competed, and where England made the longest record, France the highest, and the United States the fastest.

During the winter of 1910, France suffered greatly from terrible floods, which brought ruin to many homes, and at one time threatened to destroy a part of Paris. The soldiers were, however, immediately detailed to rescue and maintain order, and as generous contributions poured in from all sides for the sufferers, the disaster proved less great than was at first feared.

www.ingramcontent.com/pod-product-compliance
Lightning Source LLC
LaVergne TN
LVHW091258080426
835510LV00007B/307